THE COMING GUEST
and the
NEW ART FORM

THE COMING GUEST
and the
NEW ART FORM

John C. Woodcock

iUniverse LLC
Bloomington

THE COMING GUEST AND THE NEW ART FORM

iUniverse books may be ordered through booksellers or by contacting:

iUniverse LLC
1663 Liberty Drive
Bloomington, IN 47403
www.iuniverse.com
1-800-Authors (1-800-288-4677)

ISBN: 978-1-4917-3265-6 (sc)
ISBN: 978-1-4917-3266-3 (e)

Printed in the United States of America.

iUniverse rev. date: 04/30/2014

PERMISSIONS

Cover: *Old paper grunge on wood*: © Satit _Srihin—Fotolia.com

Figure 1:   *How I Ended This Summer* (2011): Scene from the movie.

Figure 2:   *Bollingen high-relief*: © Dennis L. Merritt. (2012): *The Cry of Merlin: Jung, the Prototypical Ecopsychologist.* Fisher King Press. http://www.fisherkingpress.com.

Figure 3:   *St. Matthew and the Angel*: Mikey Angels. http://en.wikipedia.org/wiki/File:Michelangelo_Merisi_da_Caravaggio_-_St_Matthew_and_the_Angel_-_WGA04127.jpg. Wikimedia Commons.

DEDICATION

The Upward Soul Gesture:

> All the soul, the coming guest, our deepest truth, needs
> is to have a real echo, a resonance in ourselves, to be
> seen, acknowledged, and appreciated for what it is.

Wolfgang Giegerich

The Downward Soul Gesture:

> The main purpose [of Jung's psychology] was the
> *incarnation of the realities of the Self.* The ego will not
> be transformed merely by experience of the imaginative
> psyche because the task is to bring the imaginative
> psyche into reality. If that equation is left suspended, if a
> route back into literal and material reality is not found,
> then nothing fundamental is ever accomplished.

Russell Lockhart

The upward soul gesture, as worked out in the psychology of
Wolfgang Giegerich, offers a methodology which requires "some
effort and poses quite a few difficulties", as with any art form.[1]
His methodology "makes soul". The practitioner of the art, if
successful, enters a soul phenomenon, (more correctly, has always
already entered it so that it becomes a soul phenomenon in the first
place—the *prime matter*), participates with its unfolding dialectical
movement, *rising up* to thinking the unity of differences where the

implicit logic (the coming guest), as which the soul phenomenon is constituted, is made explicit to the practitioner.

The downward soul gesture reflects the method of artist as "mouthpiece for the coming guest" as it seeks actualization in the real world. This method of "hearing and telling" has been inaugurated by Russell Lockhart and involves the artist's participation in the coming guest's movement down towards actualization and her enactment of its hints through "deeds"—i.e., *a doing is required.*[2]

These two soul gestures are both *necessities* (i.e. the life of soul) and this book serves to clarify the distinction between the upward gesture and the downward gesture, in order to distinguish contrasting methodologies offered by two pioneers in the field of depth psychology. As we will see, the "germ" of each methodology, so far largely overlooked by the Jungian community, originates in the same source—C. G. Jung!

This book is thus dedicated to the pioneering work of Wolfgang Giegerich and Russell Lockhart, and of course, to the lasting legacies of C. G. Jung.

PREFACE

This book is an expanded edition of my book, *The Coming Guest: Advancing Jung's Augury into the 21ˢᵗ Century* in which I first attempt to articulate my hermeneutic "reading" of Jung's little-known high relief carving at Bollingen c.1960, along with two letters he wrote, one to Sir Herbert Read and one to Dr. Tauber. In these documents I was sure I could detect the presence of "two Jungs". One was the depth psychologist whose legacy has developed into the discipline of Jungian Psychology with its various inflections. In this book, I give particular attention to *Psychology as a Discipline of Interiority* as pioneered by Wolfgang Giegerich who has refined Jung's work into a true discipline of the soul.

The other Jung was the augur-artist as I named him in yet another book, *Animal Soul*.[3] The artist Jung has also left us a legacy—one that has remained virtually unnoticed for fifty years (with one notable exception as we will see). This legacy also has its methodology—one very different from that of depth psychology. It addresses the unknown future and gives us a way to *act* that orients us to the soul background (the coming guest) of modernity, and to participate in the *event* of the incarnation of the coming guest into actuality.[4] Such participation is pre-reflective, although it may be followed by action based on reflection (memory).[5] Jung the augur-artist's legacy thus brings us close to the world-creating function of language and a new definition of the human being.[6]

CONTENTS

FOREWORD TO THE
FIRST EDITION

This is a book of analysis and auguries. As an analyst, I must apologize for my theoretical shortcomings to my several teachers who taught me how to *think*, to wield and endure the "cut" of the animus into the innocent allurement of the image. As an augur, I follow the way of "quiet whispers . . . of the signs . . . all those irrational moments when one feels the portent of the uncertain and unknown future." [2]

All my adult life I have been tossed about in the storm of that pair of opposites: the *Pontifices* and the *Augures*, which I suspect may be a true dialectical opposition. At times I have spoken *ex cathedra* (pontificating) and at others I have sounded ponderously *mysterious*, as one early teacher suggested.

I believe this pair is working through me as a dialectical opposition because, in spite of my greatest efforts, I have been unable to write exclusively in the one "voice" or the other. For example I may be writing an analytical piece and a dream will "pop up" in the middle of it, which I do not ignore. The thesis of my doctorate was written this way occasioning an interesting "invention" of a methodology to justify it. The form of literature I seem to be "doing" involves a spontaneous weaving of realities that we normally keep well apart. This writing moves from a memory to a dream to a reflection of an external event, to an etymological study of a word, to the words of another author until the usual separation of inner and outer dissolves. All my books are written this way.

If this is a living dialectic at work in my life then presumably there is a "unity of the unity and difference" implicit in these opposites I have "suffered" for so long. Until this unity is made explicit to me, no doubt books such as the one just written will strike the reader in terms of the movements between the two modes. I can only hope an underlying unity can be discerned as well.

FOREWORD TO THE
SECOND EDITION

All my books (this being my eleventh) circle around one thought:
There is almost universal understanding today that the "connective tissue" that once wove our world into a cosmos—an intelligent unity—has now disintegrated. A poet says it most eloquently in three lines:

> Turning and turning in the widening gyre
> The falcon cannot hear the falconer;
> Things fall apart; the centre cannot hold ... [8]

The frantic search to "ward off" this truth is challenged by sober logic:

> The experimental search for new symbols or a new myth that will unite everyone may certainly gather a public and create a community, but since every artist finds his own community, the particularity of such communities merely testifies to the disintegration that is taking place.[2]

Inevitability! With the collapse of absolute truth and reason as guiding principles, we are now exposed to Nietzsche's will-to-power, as our political systems demonstrate so well and, as well, desires no longer modulated by spiritual restraints are released only to be neatly exploited by our consumer industry for the purpose of selling products.[10] And so our modern civilization is slowly taking shape as an unholy union taking place between power and unconscious desire.

How are we to live in such a reality? Well, of course, as Joseph Campbell once simply remarked when asked how we are to live in a time of mythlessness, "we are doing it!" He is quite correct. Each day we get up and go about our daily lives intelligently and understandingly. This is our way of being as Daseins, as Heidegger has taught us.[11] We each simply go about our business and the world takes shape accordingly.

But according to what? Our theory of evolution tells us that the world evolves according to processes (genetic variation and environmental adaptation) that are quite independent of individual action. But in no way can such a theory account for the *shape* of our world, the form or contours it takes, now as our technological civilization. The form the world takes is the result of a union of *telos* and contingency. This "form-maker" with its *telos* was once called the soul:

> It [soul or "form-maker"—my insert] has the audacity not to be content to simply be alive, but impudently dares to have *ideas* about the world and about life itself, to insist on giving life a *telos* or *purpose*, on *interpreting* and trying to *understand* what is and what happens; it insists on *thinking*, on entertaining *fantasies* and inventing *stories*, having *memories*, perceiving the things of the world as coherent shapes and figurations; ... [12]

Like genetic evolution the word *telos* carries a meaning of necessity, "'Telos' was also an invisible bond that fate, old age, indeed death put over a person and enveloped him or her which underlines the inescapability."[13] This necessity "breaks into" the world of contingency and begins to reconfigure its shape:

> In matters of the soul process it does not matter very much whether we agree or not. It will happen anyway....
> However ... there is a great difference in *how* his [the coming guest—my insert] arrival will happen, that is to say, what it will mean for us and how it will affect us....

Thomas Mann said (in *Joseph and his Brothers*), "If you can do it, you will do it. If you cannot, it will be done to you." . . . If we resist, this reality will be mechanical and soulless. If we see the guest in it, *our* guest, indeed our deepest self, it can appear in redeemed form.[14]

C. G. Jung wrote a very similar perspective on the shape of things to come when he wrote:

[O]ur only certainty is that the new world will be something different from what we were used to. If any of his urges show some inclination to incarnate in a known shape, the creative artist will not trust it . . . he will hollow them out and hack them up. That is where we are now.[15]

And here we can get our first glimpse of how we are to live in our modern reality, this time of disintegration, chaos, and "soullessness", if we choose to serve soul.[16] Both Giegerich and Jung are speaking to the importance of how we orient ourselves to the *necessity* of the arrival of the coming guest. It matters to the outcome, to the final shape that the contours of the world assume, as configured by the union of the soul's *telos* and contingency. "Contingency" implies that we have choices, as both quotes indicate. In quoting Thomas Mann, an artist, "[i]f you can do it, you will do it. If you cannot, it will be done to you", Giegerich also aligns himself with Jung and his sense of the artist engaging or participating with the destruction of the formerly configured world and the creation of the as-yet-unknown newly configured world. There is a *doing* to be done, and that doing somehow involves the artistic impulse. This "doing" matters if the coming guest is to arrive in redeemed form or as the mechanical and soulless one that appears to be in ascendancy at this time.[17]

This book, as a further refinement of the "one thought" that underlies all my work, explores the kind of "redemptive doing" that can participate with the phenomena of the coming guest, as well as its connection with the artistic impulse. In this effort, I intend to show how the question I raised above, "how are we to live in such a reality?" can be answered—and answered with a specific methodology.

INTRODUCTION

Hans-Georg Gadamer has demonstrated the universality of hermeneutics:

> Gadamer's principal contribution to hermeneutics is to be found in his concerted effort to shift the focus of discussion away from techniques and methods of interpretation, all of which assume understanding to be a deliberate product of self-conscious reflection, to the clarification of understanding as an *event* [my italics] that in its very nature is *episodic* and *trans-subjective*. It is episodic in the sense that every particular "act" of understanding is a moment in the life of tradition itself, of which interpreter and text are subordinate parts. It is trans-subjective in that what takes place in the understanding is a mediation and transformation of past and present that transcends the knower's manipulative control.[18]

Gadamer's thought is deeply informed by the work of Martin Heidegger. In particular I would suggest that the event-character of hermeneutical understanding that Gadamer propounds springs from that most difficult of Heideggerian concepts—Ereignis:

> "Be-ing as Ereignis is history". Here 'history' does not mean the past or historical information, but the way in which be-ing and Dasein happen. To think in terms of the history of be-ing is not to tell a story about the ways be-ing has been conceived but to grasp how be-ing itself takes place. Be-ing's history must be understood

not merely in terms of change . . . but in terms of how we belong (or fail to belong) to a unique dispensation of meaning. The dispensation lays claim to us, and we can succeed or fail in laying claim to it; this dynamic of claiming, or appropriating, is crucial to the happening of be-ing.

Ereignis is the way in which the givenness of given beings—including ourselves—comes into question for us. This happening is an urgent inception that grounds a site and initiates an age that has its own unique relation to the divine.[19]

Richard Polt submits Heidegger's use of this concept to scholarly scrutiny and finds a contradiction:

[Heidegger refers to] to Ereignis as a happening and an inception or groundbreaking event. Inceptions are not "supratemporally eternal, but greater than eternity: [they are] the shocks of time".

Ereignis is now "what has always already happened before we do anything" or "the ineluctable condition of our essence . . . the way we always already are". Heidegger's writings seem to swing back and forth between two poles: unique happening and universal structures.[20]

As I now attempt to understand these quotes, I am reminded once again of Gadamer's insistence that hermeneutical understanding is an *act* in which "man *is* at all only insofar as he is addressed by being, and, in his thinking participates in the event of being. . . . Man *is* in such fashion that he is the 'there,' i.e., the illumination of being." [21]

Ereignis thus must point to a moment of self-presentation of what psychology calls the objective psyche, appearing with the phenomenology of an inception or punctum.[22] The objective psyche (soul) is the "pre-existent background" that constitutes (the form of) our historical time, our present reality. We are, in our being, always already surrounded and informed by this constitutive background: "the ineluctable condition of our essence", as Polt puts it. We come into the world already given this background which thus informs us in our comportment throughout our lives, mostly without any awareness on our part of its determining influence on our perceptions, ways of knowing etc.[23]

At times, however, for certain individuals, this already given background to our current world can break through into consciousness, i.e. break through the individual who is simply the "there" to whom being addresses itself.[24] There is a world-constituting aspect to this inception. The logical structure of the individual's prior world is brought into question and hints of a new world appear to that individual. Such a "world-shaking" event of course can initiate a psychological crisis for the individual but may, at the same time, inaugurate a new way of being. This "new way of being" is simply the slow realignment of the human being, in his or her subjective consciousness, to how he or she has always already been, in essence, simply by virtue of being born into this historical time.[25] In terms of this realignment the moment of Ereignis is thus "of the future":

> Like Aristotle's prime mover, so the work moves the artist, and works in him as an effective cause . . . . The work as that "which in the last analysis wills in him" does not drive the artist from behind, but pulls him, attracts him from the future as "the coming guest." [26]

The individual, as the "there", may comprehend "the coming new form of the soul or our Truth, and be reached and touched by it in his or her mind and heart. All the soul, the coming guest, our deepest truth, needs is to have a real echo, a resonance in ourselves, to be seen, acknowledged, and appreciated for what it is."[27]

Wolfgang Giegerich's many references to the coming guest are drawn from a now famous letter by C. G. Jung to Sir Herbert Read.[28] [29] In their discussion about the role of modern art, Jung makes reference to "the awe-inspiring guest" "knocking portentously on our door", which he also describes as "the future and picture of the new world, which we do not understand yet." Giegerich makes it very clear that, in referring to the unknown future in this way, Jung:

> . . . is not utopian thinking. Utopias present us with pictures of a better world. They want to anticipate

the future. Jung has no picture to offer. Nor does he come with a program. He comes empty-handed. He insists precisely on the future's being fundamentally unforeseeable. It cannot be anticipated. We will have to wait and see. And the question whether it will be good or bad for us is neither here nor there. We can only try to get—perhaps—a little more ready to receive it.[30]

Jung is instead referring the background movement and intelligibility of the world-constituting objective psyche:

The term "guest" is of course not a metaphoric way to refer to the new world itself with all its individual positive-factual features. Rather, this image refers to the soul of and in the new reality . . .

The guest is the new definition of the soul and of the world. Our old values, our old ideas, conceptions, expectations about what soul is and how the world is have had their day. The "ultimate values already flow towards him [the guest]," i.e., towards the new still unknown definition of the world and of the soul.

The guest whose knock on the door Jung had become aware of is thus not just a new person or new empirical phenomenon that wants to enter. It is the announcement of some new definition of the whole, a new logical status of consciousness. [31]

What is this unknown definition of the whole, a new logical status of consciousness that Giegerich is referring to here? It is clear that, for Giegerich, as for Jung, this unknown future is the mystery behind the work of the artist, "poet or seer [who] lends expression to the unspoken inner depth [or inner truth] of his time . . ."[32]:

The work [is] that "which in the last analysis wills in him", does not drive the artist from behind, but pulls him, attracts him from the future as "the coming guest." [33]

Giegerich elsewhere goes into considerable detail of the meaning of this unknown future that Jung calls the awe-inspiring guest:

> [I]t is what I term an entire "logical status," "level," or "form" of consciousness, a status or level which provides the horizon within which all particular problems will have to be addressed—in contrast to earlier ages, during which life and all the problems that came up were perceived and interpreted within the horizon of other statuses of consciousness, such as a mythological and ritualistic or a religious and metaphysical one . . . the new way of seeing life as a whole and responding to it . . . [34]

The role of the artist, in relation to the unknown future, as conceived by Giegerich seems to me to be close that of Heidegger's sense of the human being as the "there":[35]

> All that the . . . truth of the historical locus does indeed need as a human addition or contribution is that its fundamental unspokenness becomes expressed, is given articulate form, turned into a *work*, and is in this way celebrated, which is what we call soul-making. [36]

In the light of this brief introduction to 20th C. Continental philosophy and C. G. Jung's depth psychology as refined by Wolfgang Giegerich, the role of the artist in relation to the truth of our times begins to become clear.[37] The soul of our current reality is that being into which we are all "thrown" (Heidegger) and which is thus always already behind us, informing our current understanding of the world and our being in it, as seen in our very comportment (the way we understandingly conduct our lives on a daily basis). At the same time, this background is concealed from us. We do not notice our world as such (its being).[38] We simply go about our business immersed inter-subjectively with other beings in the world while, at the same time, our subjective consciousness remains immunized from the consciousness of the world (its underlying logical structure into which we are "thrown" at birth) as such. We subjectively remain "in the past", governed by personal beliefs, prejudices, conceptions etc. that belong to the truths of former times (metaphysics, religion, science).[39]

Some individuals, however, are called, or pressed upon by the new logic that already constitutes the definition of our modern world, and feel this call as from the unknown future:

> Truth as the *logos eôn* (the existing or prevailing logos) wants to be *made* true (disclosed, unconcealed), so as to become in the first place what it implicitly has been all along: *alêtheia*.[40]

Bringing the truth of our times into articulation through some cultural form is not just a hobby or leisure-time pursuit. There are consequences. Giegerich describes these consequences both in terms of the objective psyche and in terms of human beings. He begins by quoting one of Jung's favourite Greek mottos, inscribed over the entrance of his Kusnacht home: *vocatus atque non vocatus deus aderit*: "Summoned or not, the god will be here"![41]

> In matters of the soul process it does not matter very much whether we agree or not. It will happen anyway . . . . However, depending on whether the guest comes *vocatus* or whether he comes *non vocatus* there is a great difference in *how* his arrival will happen, that is to say, what it will mean for us and how it will affect us. Seneca wrote, and Jung would certainly have agreed: *Ducunt volentem fata, nolentem trahunt*, "If you are willing, fate will guide you, if you are not, it will drag you" . . . . Similarly, Thomas Mann said . . . "If you can do it, you will do it. If you cannot, it will be done to you." That's the difference. And it makes all the difference *for us*, the difference between "suffering blind victim" and "comprehending and feeling human being." But it makes also an essential difference for the arriving new reality. If we resist, this reality will be mechanical and soulless. If we see the guest in it, *our* guest, indeed our deepest self, it can appear in redeemed form.[42]

In a more acerbic passage he adds:

> One could think that the advent of the guest implies fun and joy and that the arrival of our Truth would be harmless. After all it is our own Truth. But on the contrary, the advent of our own Truth is always a terribly upsetting event. The guest is "awe-inspiring," the signs of his coming are "portentous," and "fear precedes him." The encounter with our Truth is nothing for sissies.[43]

I am one of those individuals who has been so pressed upon by the objective psyche, thus beginning a life-time's work so that the fundamental "unspokenness of our world" "becomes expressed, is given articulate form, turned into a work, and is in this way celebrated, which is what we call soul-making." [44]

Occasionally, from among the many encounters with the objective psyche that I endured over a period of twenty years or so, a jewel stands out—an inception that crystallizes all that has been said here, as well as in my books. It came in the form of a dream-vision . . .

"OUR REDEEMER"

Most dreams do not have the character of an inception. We simply wake up with a fading memory of having been "somewhere else". Some dreams, however, penetrate, shocking the dreamer into wakefulness with a feeling of "I must not forget this!" I have called such experiences "dream-visions".[45] They are self-presentational soul phenomena and the usual opposites that constitute our daily life (such as inner/outer, sleeping/awake) break down. The dream-vision simply appears! I believe such dream-visions are instances of Ereignis. Thus, one world in which I lived was brought into question and another began to knock on the door as "the coming guest":

> A man was among us, he looked quite normal, like the actor in "Cocoon" except he was alien. He was friendly, wanted to, needed to, live amongst us and was warmly welcomed. Many therapists were excited and thrilled with the glamour of his gifts, which included space ships that could fly at dizzying speeds. I joined in with this madness for a bit but lost interest and instead grew increasingly alarmed.
>
> I tried to warn others, saying, "What if . . . What if . . . ?" I decided to act, I wanted to burn him and raced around looking for a flame thrower. Instead I kept grabbing fire extinguishers and sprayed him with those—useless. He tried to stop me and we seemed to realize that there was nothing personal in this. He wanted simply to live here and I could sense incredible danger to us. I said, "It's just that our species can't survive if you stay. We need to survive too!" Then I went back to my frantic search. He said, responding to my

1

"what ifs . . .", "do you mean, what if I spit on the carpet or people?" And he did so, thus at last revealing the danger. A terrible poison was in his spittle, it dissolved flesh leaving horrible forms, like a fly dissolves its meal. I get more frantic until . . .

There is a bed of coals, so astoundingly hot that they each glow transparent red. One would simply evaporate on them. In the midst of my passion to stop the alien, a young man, a human, flings himself as a voluntary sacrifice onto the bed of coals. He is the sacrifice who will save us. I am struck with horror and agony, a religious agony that sends me to my knees as I feel his act of sacrifice. O God! O God O God! I imagine his flesh blackening and crisping as he rolls on the coals in unspeakable agony. Yet when I actually look, though I am screaming in pain and horror and awe, he is undergoing a different process. He is moving about, but in agony or intentionally, to avoid the heat or to expose himself to it?!! He is not screaming, is he in pain?

He begins to glow red just like the coal itself. He becomes transparently glowing red all over, like a clay vessel does at the highest point that forms the pot. Even more astounding, HE IS PREGNANT, ALMOST TO FULL TERM. Did he enter the ordeal that way or did the transforming fire engender a new life in him?!! By this time I cannot describe my own feelings at all. It's too much. One cannot name a mystery such as this.

He is our REDEEMER!

This dream-vision broke into consciousness in the early 1990's. At the time I was already inundated with spontaneous incursions of the psyche and all my efforts were going into recording them as best I could. I carried notebooks in my back pocket at all times, and my journals filled quickly with psychic material that I could not comprehend, although I anxiously sought amplificatory sources from the contemporary world as well as from history, and even pre-history. My psychological stability was at stake! [46]

At the time of the dream-vision I had been aware of C. G. Jung's letter to Sir Herbert Read and his image of the coming guest. So it did seem to me that the dream was showing something of the soul processes involved with this metaphor. I was most drawn at the time to the image of the young man undergoing what seemed to be a transformation through fire. For years my body had been exhibiting a chronic inflammatory condition. I was glowing red over most of my body. During the dream-vision visitation, I was literally watching this process take place in an "other" and at the same time, I was participating in the process itself.

What is this process? At the time I understood that a breakdown in logical categories was taking place and fresh perception was emerging from a new kind of logic, one that I was totally unfamiliar with: "He is moving about, but in agony or intentionally, to avoid the heat or to expose himself to it?!!" etc. I readily associated this logical breakdown with the collapse of a world, a theme that had gripped my life in so many ways at the time. I also recognized that the "alien" had something to do with technology and its world-shaking advances into every facet of our lives. Our too-easy acceptance of the "gifts" of technology was already a concern to me, as shown by several other dreams. I could further understand the "spitting" that dissolves current form and produces grotesque forms as a kind of "alien speech" that represents a threat to our current categories of thought.

These early attempts to comprehend the dream-vision were the best I could do at the time. The most important personal benefit was one of comfort, provided by the dream-vision at a time when I was bereft of any knowledgeable support from the community. It taught me that what I had believed to be only a personal psychological/physical collapse was in fact also a soul process of transformation that the ego was participating but not identical with. This discovery imbued my ordeal with meaning! I felt I could go on. My symptoms became symbolic. I knew something was happening inwardly and it was manifesting as my symptoms. I found the courage to endure as both symptoms and incursions intensified over the next several years.

TWENTY YEARS LATER

> The real meaning of a text as it addresses the interpreter
> does not just depend on the occasional factors which
> characterizer the author . . . . [I]t is always co-determined
> by the historical situation of the interpreter and thus by
> the whole course of history . . . . The meaning of a text
> surpasses its author not occasionally, but always. Thus
> understanding is not a reproductive procedure, but
> rather always also a productive one. [47]

Twenty-odd years have passed since I received that strange visitor
of the night, my "redeemer" dream-vision. It had impressed its
mostly concealed message in my heart and I slowly re-oriented my
life in a new direction. I was drawn to different literature and fresh
questions opened up new pathways. For years I forgot about the
dream and its message, but then, at times, it would reappear briefly,
like a candle flaring up in the dark. Each time I was attracted to a
different facet of the dream and followed its hints, while the dream
itself receded into darkness once more.

For example, the theme of torture arose in ascendancy along
with its curious association with ecstasy, as my dream-vision had
shown. This extraordinarily fruitful association led me to shamanic
practices of the past, in which the shaman would be tied and bound
as his spirit soared into the sky. I became fascinated by accounts
of mystical visions or poetry that had a "masochistic" quality to
them. I began to ask new questions of past practices that involved
mortification of the body. Most significantly for me, I found my
way to C. G. Jung's lectures on Nietzsche's *Zarathustra* in which
he discusses in great detail the painful psychological reality of
suspension as the process by which spiritual realities incarnate

into materiality.[48] I learned later, when his *Red Book* was published, that Jung had been most likely drawing on his own considerable experiences during his confrontation with the unconscious, in order to discuss this variant of the torture motif.[49]

Many other such avenues of study opened up for me as repercussions from this dream-vision that had occurred in the early 1990's. I was further guided through subsequent dreams that occurred over the years. In this way I entered a serious dialogue with the work of depth psychologist Wolfgang Giegerich in 1997, lasting a period of sixteen years.[50] Through his work and further dreams, I engaged intensely with 20th C. continental philosophy.[51] None of this engagement was that of a scholar—at all times I was simply exploring the questionable. My research was productive, not merely reproductive.[52]

My study of Giegerich's considerable body of work eventually took a turn that began to steer me away from other students of his psychology who seemed to advocate a more canonical interpretation of his writings.[53] I was instead intensely interested in his discussions of psychology as an art form, or his descriptions of soul as "making meaning".[54] This sense of soul, in combination with art, seemed to point to human engagement with the unknown future. When I tried to interest my colleagues with this aspect of Giegerich's writings, I felt stone-walled. Similarly my approaches to Wolfgang Giegerich himself were rebuffed very firmly. At first I was astonished, then disappointed, and then depressed. I "saw" a portcullis come down and drawbridge go up. I did not understand this reaction to my proposals at all. Any mention of future at all was excluded on principle from discussions.[55]

I felt a huge conflict within my own being. On the one hand, I knew that any understanding of modern reality and the background constitutive psyche had to include a deep understanding of Giegerich's work which privileges the soul or objective psyche as the constituting factor of world and consciousness. Yet, at the same time, he and many others seemed to reject any talk of the artist and her participation in incarnating the unknown future, or as has been described, the coming guest.[56]

I suffered this conflict for many months. Finally I pulled out all the quotes in Giegerich's books that addressed Jung, art, and the notion of the coming guest. Along with those quotes, I went to Heidegger and Gadamer, two philosophers I had been drawn to by the hints within my dreams and drank in what they had said about language, worlds, art, understanding, etc. This "brew" of fermenting thought began to work on me and I cooked! I wrote all these quotes into a single document and simply read them, cooked some more, and then re-read them. One day, as I re-opened my hermeneutical eye on the texts, I was astonished to see a detail I had not paid attention to before. Such moments are the beginning of hermeneutics, according to Gadamer. Hermeneutical understanding begins with the questionable!⁵⁷

My eyes fell on Giegerich's passage (see quote and n. 14) in which he is addresses the coming guest as the truth of our times i.e. how our present world is logically constituted. Springing from Jung's favourite motto, *vocatus atque non vocatus deus aderit,* i.e. the necessity of the incarnation of the historical soul's movements as our thus constituted world, Giegerich speaks of the difference our readiness makes to the form in which that incarnation will take: if we remain unconscious, reality will take a soulless and mechanical form but if met with feeling comprehension, i.e. seeing the "guest" in it, it can appear in *redeemed form.*

The phrase "redeemed form" hit me as a shock (the punctum—see n. 22). My redeemer dream-vision immediately surfaced again in memory and, given the context in which Giegerich's phrase occurred (my documentation of all his quotes on the coming guest), I suddenly felt free of any conflict. I comprehended the contradictions that had, up to now, pulled me in opposite directions. They were still there, but now they "belonged", just as the contradictions in my redeemer dream belonged in a totality. I now "saw" my redeemer dream with fresh eyes of new understanding. I could now see how the twenty-year old text of my dream and the concealed horizon of my present understanding were beginning to merge, disclosing more of the hidden background in which we are immersed today and which constitutes our reality.

All that remains is to articulate what I thus "saw" and at the same time how such "seeing" springs from comprehending the unity that lay beneath and within the contradictions I had felt with respect to psychology as conceived by Wolfgang Giegerich, and art as "welcoming the coming guest" i.e. the unknown future.

The alien character of the coming guest is associated in the dream with technological gifts that are naively accepted by human beings thus ushering in that "soulless and mechanical form".[58] The dream also shows the possibility of horrible or grotesque cultural forms coming into existence.[59] His appearance as a danger to us is associated in the dream with a fearful attitude and human attempts to keep him out, just as Jung shows that his appearance as a welcome guest is correlated with a human attitude of hospitality.

My wanting to burn him with fire to get rid of the threat seems to be an image of an intuition that fire is somehow involved in the process of incarnation (his wanting to come and live among us) but simply *using* fire to remove the threat is thwarted (fire becoming fire extinguishers) and the danger intensifies (the speech that produces grotesque forms). The conflicts involved in this first movement of engaging the coming guest intensify to a climax, the image of which is fire reaching a maximum peak of heat (the burning coals). It seems that if a voluntary human sacrifice is made by one who chooses to throw himself unreservedly into this cultural conflict, going beyond the obsolete way of being (a world constituted in terms of subject-object relations, i.e. metaphysics), he will enter a fluid state of being that is the logic of our presently constituted technological civilization. In this way he becomes able to participate in the soul movement (the coming guest) and a very different form of incarnation becomes possible (the pregnancy)—a future form, born from within the present human being, that the dream-vision calls "redeemed": a new definition of the human being correlative to the logic that nonetheless always already constitutes our modern world.[60]

I think Wolfgang Giegerich is saying something very similar when he says:

> The word "vocatus" in the *vocatus atque non vocatus* adage therefore does not mean that we would have to *wish for* and try our best to *promote* the new world of technology and the anaesthetized mind or any other positive-factual features of this development. All it means is to see "the guest" *in* the technological development and respect him as such.[61]

John C. Woodcock

Giegerich rightly insists that the future is fundamentally unforeseeable, yet at the same time, there is "something" to "see", i.e., the guest within technological development. This guest is therefore both the concealed soul life that always already constitutes our modern world and, at the same time, the "work . . . [which] does not drive the artist from behind, but pulls him, attracts him from the future as "the coming guest." Giegerich goes further to define the coming guest as "the new definition of the soul and of the world."[62]
Giegerich is saying here that the coming guest is the background logic that is always already behind us, informing human conduct and understanding in our modern world. It is also our unforeseeable future which, as such, can pull on the artist in order to say itself into existence through an artistic or cultural form. He specifies much further than these hints:

> "[T]he *real* problem" of the future will be a psychological one . . . [Psychology] is what I term an entire "logical status," "level," or "form" of consciousness, a status or level which provides the horizon within which all particular problems will have to be addressed—in contrast to earlier ages, during which life and all the problems that came up were perceived and interpreted within the horizon of other statuses of consciousness, such as a mythological and ritualistic or a religious and metaphysical one . . . . Psychology [is] the new way of seeing life as a whole and responding to it, psychology as the successor formation to mythology, religion, and metaphysics.[63]

Giegerich makes clear here (and indeed throughout his works) that such statements are not those of an advocate privileging one discipline over any other. Such a misinterpretation of Giegerich's statement here would fly in the face of his insistence that the future in its positive-factual form is completely unforeseeable. No, Giegerich is talking about the soul in its historical self-transformations. His reference is to the soul background or that which constitutes our world in the first place and gives us our current understanding "from behind" as it were, in complete

8

agreement with Gadamer's insight into the universality of hermeneutics i.e., our understanding as beings-in-the-world.[64]

Mythology, religion and metaphysics are now academic disciplines but were formerly *ways* of knowing (i.e. knowing the truth of their times) that were made possible only as informed by the world-constituting status of soul-life that lay behind and within them.[65] Giegerich has laboured for decades to work out this complex relationship between historical cultural forms and the logical status of soul-being that, from behind, constitutes each historical time as such.[66] It is only from a relatively deep study of his work that one could, I think, come to understand what he means by claiming that the coming guest, as intuited by Jung, is psychology, "the new way of seeing life as a whole and responding to it, psychology as the successor formation to mythology, religion, and metaphysics." It is the new status of soul-being, the "form-maker" of our modern technological civilization, which informs our current ways of knowing, making psychology possible in the first place, as a modern discipline.[67]

We already exist as psychological beings in this new sense. As beings-in-the-world we always already comport ourselves understandingly in the world, by virtue of the new status of soul, informing such understanding from behind and within. We do so, however, while our subjective consciousness remains immune to such understanding.[68] We are thus psychologically constituted today as a dissociated form of consciousness.

Although this new status of soul lies concealed within our psychological being, Giegerich is explicit about its logical structure. He calls this structure the psychological difference and it is the truth of our times![69] We humans, as speaking beings that constitute our world linguistically, already exist as this psychological structure but, as Giegerich says throughout his works, we do so neurotically. We know full well that we have left one formerly constituted world and are now inhabiting a new world yet we deny what we know and cling instead to beliefs and attitudes that we know are logically obsolete, belonging to former ages, such denial being of course the very definition of neurosis.[70]

As the truth of our times, the psychological difference is therefore the coming guest i.e., the logical status of soul that constitutes the form of the world today. It is also that which pulls the artist, attracting him or her from the future.

It was this formulation of the coming guest that ended the conflict between my horizon of understanding and the texts of Wolfgang Giegerich. In the very manner of generation of productive meaning, when the event of hermeneutics occurs, I was now confronted with two questions that spontaneously emerged from my understanding:

1. As the coming guest is always already behind and within the forms of our technological civilization, what real phenomena *can* become its self-display? In other words, can we discern the psychological difference behind and within given modern phenomena?

2. The second question concerns the artist today who is pulled by the coming guest as the unknown future, seeking incarnation through the artist. What form of art would we look towards today as an adequate vehicle that can give birth to the coming guest in "material" form, thus participating in a process of incarnation?

I will now attempt to respond to the first of these two questions.

THREE SOUL PHENOMENA
AND THE COMING GUEST

Not all modern phenomena are soul phenomena for our present form of consciousness i.e. hints of the coming guest. One of Heidegger's many great discoveries and conceptions is that of the phenomenology of things. He has shown that, in past historical times, a thing, by its very nature, gathered a world to it, so that is became expressive of that world.[21] In former times, for example, weapons gathered ritual practice around them, which disclosed an entire way of being of a people. We could think of the American Indian pipe in this regard with its originating myth well-known to the people and its required ritual practices. Equipment possessed soul-life and was to be handled only by its owner. Mistakes in this regard required ritual reparation.

In our modern world, however, our technological civilization, Heidegger has successfully shown how things have been stripped of this gathering and have thus become resources only:

> They are no one's because they are everyone's. Their
> nature, one might say, is to have only a general nature,
> a nature exhausted by their impersonal usefulness
> to any one of us. Or, to put it more precisely, all these
> things are entities the being of which fails to gather the
> manifold conditions of their coming to presence.[22]

In terms of psychology as a discipline of interiority, we can say that soul life has departed the things of today and they thus are no longer ensouled in their thingness. They cannot become soul phenomena (i.e. in their "eachness") and thus disclose the coming guest. The soul is now the inwardness or interiority of language, not things. Heidegger describes it this way, as interpreted by Edwards:

> Technology is a way—according to Heidegger, it is now the fundamental way—in which the world of human beings is revealed, constituted, and populated: it is an over-arching set of linguistic and behavioral practices that allow our entities to appear around us in a particular way, that give to the entities that appear in our world a particular being, a particular significance, a particular sense.[23]

We must, in our modern world linguistically constituted as it is, turn to language as the only phenomenon whose inwardness or soul may self-disclose as the coming guest.[24]

With this prior understanding, I found my way to three modern linguistic forms that opened up for me as soul phenomena and thus became hints of the coming guest as the psychological difference. They thus disclosed the truth of our times, i.e. the constituting factor that makes possible our particular way of being today.

The first soul phenomenon is a news report. In San Francisco recently (2013), a man got on the train and began to casually wave a gun around. Video cameras afterwards showed that he was carelessly looking for a random victim. Finally, as a young man moved to the exit, the killer found his mark, and as the young man stepped on to the platform, he was shot dead. As the story unfolded in the news, the most shocking aspect that was being reported was the fact that nobody had noticed this man who was so obviously waving his gun around for many minutes as he, radar-like, honed in on his as yet unknown victim.

Where was everybody else on this crowded subway? They were, in one sense, sitting right there, next to the killer. At the same time they were somewhere else—absorbed in their iPods, phones, Blackberries etc. This fact is what shocked the reporter.

As I was listening intently to this alarming report, I made a shift to the "within". The story was now a soul phenomenon. Associations began to gather, as attracted by the soul phenomenon itself, not by my subjectivity.

I cannot in this short space describe the rich nest of images and thoughts that emerged as I "became pregnant" with this story (now as reflected, i.e. as mindedness, soul). What I can do here is, in a more deliberate fashion, try to articulate how this soul phenomenon became understood by me as a self-display of the psychological difference, as this living concept actualized itself through the lives of those people on the subway, and therefore perhaps contributing to the death of this young man.

The people on the subway were sitting, standing, or leaning, in their customary manner. Some indeed probably saw this killer waving his gun around. They got in and out of the train, adjusted their coats, ate chocolate bars, and listened to their technological devices. They thus inhabit the same world as we all do: that world of background intelligibility that Heidegger has shown to be the world of Dasein, our way of understanding and coping in a pre-reflective manner. [25]

At the same time, we inhabit another world, one that renders us immune to the consciousness of the world of Dasein. This other world we inhabit is reflected in our daily use of technological devices but we must be careful here in our description. These devices can be seen simply as Heidegger's ready-to-hand, i.e. the equipment that we use in such a way as to reveal the background intelligibility of the world of Dasein. For example, I may use an iPod, my laptop, and then my iPhone during the subway journey, all as equipment in Heidegger's sense: if used in connection with one another and in the larger context of my activities that day, they together reveal my pre-reflective understanding, my ordinary way of intelligently coping, say, as a modern business man embedded in the world of business.

Crucially, technological devices can also be seen from the soul's point of view whereupon their "thingness" or "appearance as equipment" (Heidegger's "occurrence" and "ready-to-hand") are not and can no longer be ensouled. [26] Rather they may be seen at best as indicators, or instances that can point us to the life of the soul today, which "appears" as the living thinking that gives rise to our technological civilization in the first place. [27] We are psychologically embedded in this world that we call our technological civilization. [28] We do not have to be using technological devices to "be in this world". As a matter of course, we psychologically live "out in space" where we gaze upon the empirical world or "environment", a perspective that was impossible for our forebears who were embedded in an ensouled world, appearing as enchanted nature, or nature as a text, for example. The modern soul may be discerned, not as image, but as the "invisible syntax" informing our every-day speech, as we language our world.

In an almost perfunctory manner we speak the world as way below us, a world upon which we commonly make pronouncements, judgments, decisions, and take actions on behalf of. Global warming, environmental factors, world court, macroeconomics, world population, are but a small sample of the way we commonly language our psychological world today. Within such language, we may discern a consciousness that is exterior to and above the world-as-a-whole. Our search for and enthusiasm for wholes, or totalities, or unity, springs from this source. We no longer concern ourselves with individual entities but only the totality. For example we easily replace one iPod with another but have grave fears for any sign of the Internet crashing. It's the same with people—I can feel, on the empirical individual level, how utterly unimportant I am, while at the same time we all share anxieties about the end of our entire species.

In other words, this simple, though distressing, report of a dreadful, but all-too-common incident in our ordinary lives today reveals that soul (psychological life) has long departed the world of things, which has thus become Heidegger's world of Dasein.

We thus inhabit two worlds simultaneously. The world of background intelligibility for most people does not include gun-waving murderers. Although the passengers undoubtedly saw the gun, they only saw it as occurrent, in Heidegger's terms, a mere item that in-itself carries no meaning. It was not part of their ready-to-hand, their equipment, so to speak. They thus could take no intelligible action. We could suggest that for a military person, on the other hand, the gun would appear as equipment (a ready-to-hand) and he would therefore know what to do next. The gun's meaning would be self-evident, as revealing the intelligibility of the world of the military.

The psychological world of our technological civilization certainly does include guns etc. as its equipment but these guns are virtual. Every game player would know exactly what to do if a virtual gun is displayed in a game, or as an icon etc. However, the empirical world is now externalized and cannot therefore engage us psychologically, although, as Daseins, we can and do cope quite successfully in that world, except when, as above, there is an appearance that intrudes into that world and is not part of its ready-to-hand (equipment that can be related to intelligently).

This incident, as reflected in my mind, thus shows how we can live in two worlds simultaneously, with one having nothing to do with the other—a dissociation! This is what Wolfgang Giegerich means by the psychological difference as a living concept, thinking itself out through our actual lives, sometimes, as we see, with tragic consequences. [79]

Now we can turn to another (what became for me) soul phenomenon in order to explore the psychological difference from another angle: can there be a soul phenomenon that displays the psychological difference in action in our lives, in terms of a break-down of the dissociation (collapse of a world)? As before, my final description is a re-worked version of the experience of "becoming pregnant with" or "interiorizing myself into" the soul phenomenon, so that *it* could speak (in image, or thinking).

The second soul phenomenon disclosive of the psychological difference was a movie which starkly demonstrates our modern mode of living as an expression of the psychological difference, this time becoming "visible" through a breakdown in the dissociation: [80]

> On a desolate island in the Arctic Circle, two men work at a small meteorological station, taking readings from their radioactive surroundings. Sergei, a gruff professional in his fifties, takes his job very seriously. His new partner, bright eyed college grad Pavel, retreats to his MP3 player and video games to avoid Sergei's imposing presence. One day while Sergei is out, inexperienced Pavel receives terrible news for Sergei from HQ. Intimidated, Pavel can't bring himself to disclose the information. When the truth is finally revealed, the consequences explode against a chilling backdrop of thick fog, sharp rocks, and the merciless Arctic Sea. [81]

This synopsis places the human beings at the centre, making the plot a human story set "against a chilling backdrop of thick fog, sharp rocks, and the merciless Arctic Sea". However, this movie appeared to me as a soul phenomenon, i.e., I felt it held a hint of soul movement, and I gave myself over to it.

Gazing at the photo above, I immediately saw the figure physically surrounded by the chilling, inhospitable Arctic ice and rock. But wait! He is wearing head-phones. He is listening to some rock music. Although he is physically rather a small frail figure, in a wilderness of ice, psychologically he is quite dissociated from all that:

> The person with the walkman seems to move through the real world: he is sitting in a tram, he does his homework, he is jogging through nature, and yet in actuality he is totally enwrapped in the music coming at a deafening volume from his walkman and, as far as the soul (not the ego) is concerned, shielded from the external world. One must not be misled by the external impression that the person with a walkman is in the outside world and as ego may be fully aware of it. In truth, i.e. psychologically, he is inside the hermetically sealed world of sound, swallowed by it . . . [82]

The entire purpose of the two men's stay in the Arctic is scientific. They are there to collect data from helioscopes. They have radio isotope generators nearby and computers inside the station. They must convert this data into telemetry that can be compared with that from other stations. Each man psychologically is a physicist. They each are relating to the outside world as bits of data. In other words, for them as psychological beings, the world exists as content within their consciousness. They in their consciousness surround the world. They are above the world, like satellites and the world appears to them as a digitalized content. For example, their interest in the sun lies solely in its appearing to them in the form of data gathered up by the helioscopes. We must not be fooled by apparent engagements with nature such as the older man's going fishing. The fish to him are simply produce, to be gathered, salted, and brought home to his wife. There is no hint of a relationship of say, worship, or ritual killing requiring an act of propitiation to the "Master fish", as happened in the original tribal methods of hunting.

Animals and indeed the men's own physical bodies as animals, only exist as empirical objects (Heidegger's occurrences—see above) for these two men, in their psychological existence, and indeed so it is for us in our modern form of existence. This may be seen quite clearly in the older man's complete disregard for his own, or the younger man's physical being. There was no music, no comfort, and no discussions taking place in the station that may have "warmed the hearts." There was simply sleeping between broadcasts of the ever-demanding telemetry, which clearly dictated the terms of their existence. Their lives in the station expressed the cold, abstract, utterly alien character of the telemetric data.

The cost of this dissociated consciousness as which we exist today begins to emerge in the movie through the disintegration of the world of the physicist and his data (the inverted, digitalized natural world). This was accomplished dramatically through increasing increments of fear and mistrust in the younger man as he sensed his utter dependency on the older man who was rather brutal in his manner. Each man descended from his lofty realm of abstractions where he felt purposeful, authoritative, knowledgeable, etc., back to earth where animal survival once again prevailed as it once did for our ancestors.

Unlike our ancestors however, there is now no soul life reflecting itself in nature, which the men could rely on for wisdom, guidance, and perhaps ritual preparation for death. Nature therefore became a terrifying alien presence! Nature once embraced us, contained us, and provided meaning to us. No more! Nature now reflected back the degree to which we have become alien in our existence to nature. Brute survival enwrapped in terror was all that was left, as one man set about murdering the other.

Our modern status as psychological beings totally alien to nature is captured very well in the dramatic moment of the men finally leaving the station and going back home to the city—a move totally impossible and unthinkable for our ancestors who were surrounded by nature in its living presence at all times in their existence.

Although the status of our modern consciousness did not come home to our protagonists, the movie does show us the dissociation in stark dramatic form, as it begins to break down.

We may see from these two modern soul phenomena how we can discern the psychological difference as a real background factor determining our human lives today. The soul has always been the determining background to our world and, as it goes through its historical self-transformations, we correspondingly find ourselves (as already being) in new worlds.[83] Our world today is thus determined by the present soul-structure which is one of a self-dissociation (the psychological difference).

Once we know of the reality and truth of the psychological difference, can we live it consciously? That is, can I exist authentically, to borrow Heidegger's term?[84] [85]

A passage by Wolfgang Giegerich may shed light on the question of *living the reality* of the psychological difference in a way that echoes, or resonates with the truth of our times.[86] He refers to the psychological difference in terms of what he calls natural Being (when the world was constituted as "living nature") and the New Being of our technological world civilization. We are in now between these two worlds, and as such, we can prevent dissociation between them by preserving a feeling relation to the *rage* that indicates the soul's leave-taking of natural Being as the soul moves into the status of its New Being, while at the same time, *preparing* ourselves for the New Being, the contours of which remain unknown. Such a stance, according to Giegerich, would lead us into a capacity for modesty, self-irony, melancholy, and love!

I had a shock of recognition when I read this passage. In 1994, I had had another dream-vision, the impact of which, along with my "redeemer" dream-vision, has shaped my life ever since. This dream-vision is the third soul phenomenon that I want to discuss here as displaying the coming guest in stark form.

I simply "saw" an image of natural Being (goddess) destroying itself in an apocalypse of rage-terror, as the technological civilization gains hold as the New Being. Crucially, as we will see, the dream shows that the soul is negating itself. The "goddess" is bringing about her own destruction. The Old Being gives way to the New.

As I participated with the agony of "her" rage-despair, I became pregnant with a poem which burst through! It seems to me even today that this poem expresses the soul movement that Wolfgang Giegerich describes above: always "carrying the weight of the furies" as we become truly human, with understanding and love. The dream-vision begins:

> I am working at a thermonuclear facility along with others. It is the central facility of our society. It is regulated and master minded by central computer, much like HAL in 2001, even to the detail of the Red Eye with which we could communicate. This computer however is female. Everybody thought of her as an IT! In contrast I would look into her eye and talk to HER, subject to subject, with love. In other words, the feminine regulating principle which is the glue of society, by relating all parts to one another and to the whole has become an IT!
>
> But my response alone is not enough. Slowly the lack of relatedness begins to drive her mad with grief. At first this shows with an increasing, dangerous autonomy in the operation of the objects associated with the facility (society): elevators going sideways, doors opening and shutting autonomously, etc. Then people began to harm one another in various ways until the social system became frayed and anarchy increases

with civilization and its values losing cohesion and crumbling.

I find myself in a garbage dump, near the central facility. Some abandoned children give me a gun to kill them. I take it away from them. A vagabond is sitting in an abandoned car, sewing a boot for the coming (nuclear?) winter. He also used to work in the facility, he says. A sick woman careens by. A man tries to take his twin boys up a tower.

Now I am standing at the centre of the facility. It is Ground Zero, a large cleared area of gray sand and dirt with concentric rings, like a target, radiating from the centre. The ground is slightly raised at the centre, like a discus, sloping away to the edges. I sense that she is going to explode. I am right at the epicentre. She is going to destroy us all and this means herself in an apocalypse of rage, despair, loathing, hate and grief because of our stupidity.

I must get away from the epicentre now. I sprint across the field, down the slight incline to the periphery of the field and sprawl prone, with my head facing the centre, just as she explodes.

The wind starts from the centre and blows out (in contrast to the natural phenomenon which sucks up). It begins as a breeze, increasing in strength and intensity until it becomes an unbearable shriek. Lying face down, I am sheltered by the slope as the wind rips over my back. But I mustn't raise my head at all, a few inches of protection and that's it! Then I know the shriek is hers. I "see" her standing at the centre and a poem burst spontaneously from my lips:

The goddess
Flowing
In her agony.
Awesome!
Incomparable grief and rage
Divine suffering
Excruciating pain

> Such terrible agony
> Beauty, sublime beauty
>
> How is love possible?
> Yet this is what I feel.

A bubble of calm forms around me while the storm of destruction rages on outside. She is with me in a form that I can talk to. The bubble makes our conversation sound like a small echo chamber. She tells me that because I loved her I may have the boy back (Christopher?). I say, "O! Do you want me in exchange?" I feel quite calm and composed about this. She says No, no exchange, just a gift. Then the bubble collapses and the wind shrieks again. Gradually it dissipates and as I tumble over, feeling its last tendrils whip at my clothes, I find myself tumbling out of this scene into the everyday world of my daily life. I have been returned from a visionary place to my ordinary life. Then I wake up.[87]

Earlier I had quoted Giegerich suggesting the task of modern men and women:

> We can only try to get—perhaps—a little more ready to receive it [the coming guest]. The word "vocatus in the vocatus atque non vocatus" adage therefore does not mean that we would have to wish for and try our best to promote the new world of technology and the anaesthetized mind or any other positive-factual features of this development. All it means is to see "the guest" in the technological development and respect him as such.[88]

My goddess dream-vision self-presents, within its imagery, the coming guest as the psychological difference, very close to Wolfgang Giegerich's description quoted above. It further shows that, if the human being can endure the dissociation consciously as it works itself out, then a new birth takes place: love is born in the human heart and expressed in poesis! Comprehension of the psychological difference involves a gesture of rising up to the logical status of soul today, being able to hold the contradiction in the heart without dissociating. Crucially though, there appears to be a counter-gesture on the part of soul to descend into that human heart and, by way of pregnancy and birth, give rise to a new form of love via enactment in the sense that Russell Lockhart means:

> The "great Dream" [the coming guest—my insert] is born from following, submitting to, humbling oneself and one's ego to the hint of the dream: *to act on the hint of the dream.* An eros relation to the dream must lie in enacting the dream's hint . . . . In this lies the "picture and future of the new world". Jung says we do not understand it yet . . . . [T]he eros of enactment generates meaning through doing and the consequences of doing . . . . It is not a matter of knowledge of even of consciousness . . . [89]

Elsewhere, Lockhart describes the process of enactment in relation to the coming guest, by reference to the author, Margaret Atwood:

> Rather than seeking after the dream's meaning, we can ask ourselves instead what we will do differently today as a result of this dream. In this way we get closer to the inner workings of the dream. The imagination actually becomes engaged with the dream. Here is a clear example from the writer Margaret Atwood:
>
> *The best writing dream I ever had was in the mid-Sixties. I dreamt I'd written an opera about a nineteenth-century English emigrant called Susanna Moodie, whose account of her awful experiences, "Roughing It In The Bush", was among my parents' books. It was a very emphatic dream, so I researched Mrs. Moodie, and eventually wrote a poem sequence, a television play, and a novel—Alias Grace—all based on material found in her work.*
>
> To be sure, we are not writers of Atwood's stature. But that is not the point. The point is that she acted

on the dream. Notice that in the dream she writes an opera. But as a result of acting on the dream, she ends up writing a poem, a television play and a novel. She might have stopped herself from doing anything at all with the dream if she had focused on "I can't" write an opera. So "acting on a dream" is not literally doing what the dream says, but following the hints embodied in the imagination that is prompted by the dream, which in this case, led to a poem, a TV play, and a novel. These particular things were not previously envisioned as part of Atwood's future, but they "became" her future out of her actions in relation to the story of the dream.[20]

In examining the work of Wolfgang Giegerich and Russel Lockhart, both Jungian psychologists, as they each approach the question of human response to the truth of our times, i.e., the coming guest, I could see just how close they are in their thinking and valorising Jung's great premonition concerning the "picture and future of the new world" while, at the same time, emphasising opposite gestures in a methodological response to that premonition.

Here we are getting close to the meaning of the lines quoted in my Dedication. Wolfgang Giegerich emphasises the importance of human beings rising up to the level of soul today in its logical structure as the psychological difference, his particular formulation of the truth of our times: "All it means is to see "the guest" in the technological development and respect him as such." Lockhart affirms this gesture but at the same time, acknowledges another opposite soul movement that involves "enacting the dream's hint", understood as an eros act that can spring from comprehension or intuition of the coming guest only when the human being is in a state whereby she can choose consciously to so act.

We can see their closeness in thought and difference in gesture as being two inflections springing from an original "double gesture" that is expressed in a little-known "text" of C. G. Jung's late thought. This double gesture is his legacy to us and as we shall see, points us to the answer to my second question (see previous chapter):

What form of art would we look towards today as an adequate vehicle that can give birth to the coming guest in "material" form, thus participating in a process of incarnation?

JUNG'S DOUBLE LEGACY

While we are quite aware of Jung's enduring legacy as the pioneer of Analytical Psychology, a legacy that has profoundly changed the lives of others, there is a lesser known but equally important legacy of his work.[21]

We can see the seeds of this hidden legacy lying quietly within three documents of the soul that Jung "bequeathed" us c. 1960, one year before he died. Together these documents constitute the "text" that, as we will see, reveals the soul's double gesture in relation to the coming guest.

The first is his famous letter to Sir Herbert Read in 1960, a letter that reveals Jung's attitude towards art and artists. Here is the portion relevant to our discussion here:

> The great problem of our time is that we don't understand what is happening to the world. We are confronted with the darkness of the soul, the unconscious. It sends up its dark and unrecognizable urges. It hollows out and hacks up the shapes of our culture and its historical dominants. We have no dominants any more, they are in the future. Our values are shifting, everything loses it certainty . . . . Who is the awe-inspiring guest who knocks at our door portentously? Fear precedes him, showing that ultimate values already flow towards him . . . our only certainty is that the new world will be something different from what we were used to. If any of his urges show some inclination to incarnate in a known shape, the creative artist will not trust it . . . he will hollow

them out and hack them up. That is where we are now. They have not yet learned to discriminate between their wilful mind and the objective manifestation of the psyche . . . . If the artist of today could only see what the psyche is spontaneously producing and what he, as a consciousness, is inventing, he would notice that the dream f.i. or the object is pronouncing (through his psyche) a reality from which he will never escape, because nobody will ever transcend the structure of the psyche.[22]

I will return to this letter, so laden with hints for the future as it is, but now the second document of the soul that I want to introduce is a carving Jung produced on the wall of his retreat at Bollingen c. 1960:[93]

This carving, as a document of the soul, has lain virtually mute for fifty years, with one significant exception. Deep within its surface pictures, more seeds of Jung's hidden legacy lie quietly, perhaps only now ready to germinate.[24]

The third document of the soul that belongs here with the other two is a letter written by Jung to Dr. Tauber, at the end of 1960 in which he attempts to address Tauber's request for understanding in relation to the carving:

> Many thanks for your kind suggestion that I write a commentary on my Bollingen symbols. Nobody is more uncertain about their meaning than the author himself. They are their own representation of the way they came into being.
>
> The first thing I saw in the rough stone was the figure of the worshipping woman, and behind her the silhouette of the old king sitting on his throne. As I was carving her out, the old king vanished from view. Instead I suddenly saw that the unworked surface in front of her clearly revealed the hindquarters of a horse, and a mare at that, for whose milk the primitive woman was stretching out her hands. The woman is obviously my anima in the guise of a millennia-old ancestress.
>
> Milk, as *lac virginis*, virgin's milk, is a synonym for the *aqua doctrinae* . . . . The mare descending from above reminded me of Pegasus. Pegasus is the constellation above the second fish in Pisces; it precedes Aquarius in the precession of the equinoxes. I have represented it in its feminine aspect, the milk taking the place of the spout of water in the sign for Aquarius. This feminine attribute indicates the unconscious nature of the milk. Evidently the milk has first to come into the hands of the anima, thus charging her with special energy.
>
> This afflux of anima energy immediately released in me the idea of a she-bear, approaching the back of the anima from the left. The bear stands for the savage energy and power of Artemis. In front of the bear's forward-striding paws I saw, adumbrated in the stone, a ball, for a ball is often given to bears to play with in the bear-pit. Obviously this ball is being brought to the worshipper as a symbol of individuation. It points to the meaning or content of the milk.
>
> The whole thing, it seems to me, expresses coming events that are still hidden in the archetypal realm. The

anima, clearly, has her mind on spiritual contents. But
the bear, the emblem of Russia, sets the ball rolling.
Hence the inscription: *Ursa movet molem.* [25]

Within these three documents of the soul we can discern the
soul's double gesture with respect to art and the coming guest.
Wolfgang Giegerich has refined one aspect of this gesture into
his psychology, a method and art form that allows us to bring
to consciousness the logical life that constitutes our modern
technological civilization, disclosing to us how we exist as that
logical life (psychological difference, coming guest); while Russell
Lockhart has developed the other aspect of the soul's double gesture
into a new art form of erotic enactment which proclaims and
welcomes the coming guest, with love, into material form.

Both aspects become clear in Jung's approach to his carving on
the wall at Bollingen, each being fundamentally different in intent
and method!

The soul gestures can best be seen as described or hinted at in
the letters to Read and later, to Tauber.

The upward gesture may be discerned within *psychologist* Jung's
approach when faced with any already formed document of the soul
("dead letter").[26] This approach or methodology is well understood
in the depth psychological community and combines two aspects—
that of archetypal amplification ("Pegasus" etc.) and reductive
interpretation ("my anima" etc.). I will extract the passages that
show this most clearly in his letter to Tauber:

> On the left the bear, symbol of the savage strength
> and energy of Artemis, is moving the mass . . . . An
> allusion to Russia or the Russian bear which gets
> things rolling . . . A primitive woman reaches out for
> the milk of the mare . . . . My anima in the guise of a
> millennia-old ancestress . . . The mare . . . Reminded me
> of Pegasus . . . the milk taking the place of the spout
> of water . . . . The feminine attribute indicates the
> unconscious nature of the milk . . . . The ball is brought
> to the worshipper as a symbol of individuation. It points
> to the meaning and content of the milk.

Both these methods, as used by Jung here, leave the human mind in abstractions, an upward gesture. Nothing material is produced from such methods.

The downward gesture of soul, on the other hand, can be discerned within *artist* Jung's method while he is forming what will *later* become a "dead letter" (already formed)—i.e. the carving. His approach may be more easily seen if we extract the relevant passages from both letters: This method consists in bringing into existence hints or portents of the unknown future as it forms itself through the artist:

To Read:

> We are confronted with the darkness of our soul . . . .
> It sends up its dark and unrecognizable urges . . .
> everything loses its certainty . . . . If any of his urges
> show some inclination to incarnate in a known shape,
> the creative artist will not trust it . . . he will hollow
> them out and hack them up . . .

To Tauber:

> Many thanks for your kind suggestion that I write a
> commentary on my Bollingen symbols. Nobody is more
> uncertain about their meaning than the author himself.
> They are their own representation of the way they came
> into being.
>
> The first thing I saw in the rough stone was the
> figure of the worshipping woman, and behind her the
> silhouette of the old king sitting on his throne. As I
> was carving her out, the old king vanished from view.
> Instead I suddenly saw that the unworked surface
> in front of her clearly revealed the hindquarters of a
> horse, and a mare at that, for whose milk the primitive
> woman was stretching out her hands . . . . This afflux of
> anima energy immediately released in me the idea of a
> she-bear, approaching the back of the anima from the
> left . . . . In front of the bear's forward-striding paws I
> saw, adumbrated in the stone, a ball . . .

Jung had a lifetime of scholarship and knowledge of symbols behind him as he turned to the already formed carving for an interpretation. He was not lacking in his capacity to amplify almost any symbol. Interestingly then, when it came to his own production of the carving at Bollingen he admitted his ignorance and even had to distort the actual imagery in order to amplify and interpret, this being evidence that there was too much unknown in the carving for him to understand. The distortion was also in the face of his oft-quoted dictum—"stick to the image", which means that every soul phenomenon has all that it needs within itself in order to self-disclose its meaning!

In particular, we can focus on his distortion of the image of the mare which he interpreted as a feminine aspect of Pegasus, the milk taking the place of the gushing inspirational waters of Hippocrene which were released by the flashing hoof of Pegasus, striking the rocks of hardened traditional forms. This interpretive move to Pegasus did however begin to release the meaning of the carving as having to do with our present time of chaos, conceived by Jung as that time between the Age of Pisces and the coming Age of Aquarius[27]—a time in which "the darkness of the soul, the unconscious . . . sends up its dark and unrecognizable urges. It hollows out and hacks up the shapes of our culture and its historical dominants."

It took the sensitive work of another psychologist, in 1982, to "clean up" the amplifications and render the meaning of the carving more explicit, particularly by staying closer to the image of mare.

Russell Lockhart's remarkable little book, *Psyche Speaks: A Jungian Approach to Self and World*, in 1987 was the fruit of his inaugural lectures (C. G. Jung lecture series) given in New York by invitation of the C. G. Jung Foundation for Analytical Psychology in 1982. The lectures and book are essentially a work of whispers and silence, hints and auguries, thus charting new territory for Jungian thought—territory that, like Jung's augury carved in rock has largely remained hidden in darkness until the present time.

Lockhart gave a good deal of attention to Jung's carving and its meaning in this little book. Perhaps the interval of (then) twenty odd years prepared the way to a clearer, less distorted amplification of the "mare" image, which in turn, has brought the meaning of the augury more fully into visibility.

Lockhart remained faithful to Jung's dictum "stick to the image" and to his method of amplification which is applied to contents that are difficult to understand, for the sake of elucidation of the meaning so that it may yield itself more easily to our understanding. After speaking about Pegasus for a while, particularly the rich associations of poetry and inspiration, Lockhart goes on to say:

> Even more directly we know that the great *goddess* of poetry and inspiration was pictured as a mare goddess, and her nurturant milk was the source of inspiration. Her name was *Aganippe*, a name which is related to words for "madness" and "night-mare." . . . What the psyche is seeking in the transition from the Picean to the Aquarian age is the waters of Hippocrene, the milk Aganippe, of poetic madness, the source and nurse of inspiration. It is the voice of this inspired psyche, the psyche nursed by the milk of the Muses, that catches the ear of the artist soul and through the many acts of bringing forth creates that welcoming song to the coming guest. It caught Jung's eye, and he pictured it in stone.[28]

Jung became an artist as he participated in the production of the carving at Bollingen or as the images emerged into materiality through him. Hear once again how it happened from Jung's letter to Tauber (with Jung's subsequent interpretations removed):

> The first thing I saw in the rough stone was the figure of the worshipping woman, and behind her the silhouette of the old king sitting on his throne. As I was carving her out, the old king vanished from view. Instead I suddenly saw that the unworked surface in front of her clearly revealed the hindquarters of a horse, and a mare at that, for whose milk the primitive woman was stretching out her hands . . . . This afflux of anima energy immediately released in me the idea of a she-bear, approaching the back of the anima from the

left . . . . In front of the bear's forward-striding paws I
saw, adumbrated in the stone, a ball . . .

Understanding has no place here, whereas enactment surely
does. Lockhart is demonstrating how Jung the artist, in *carving* the
high-relief, was in fact enacting what he, Jung, was at the same time,
auguring, as shown in the images produced—the new art form as
welcoming the coming guest into materiality.

Giegerich carefully distinguishes the work of the artist who
welcomes the coming guest from other forms of art. From his
perspective of the soul, certain human beings participate in the
soul's historical self-transformations which lie behind and within
our thus constituted world. These human beings have broadened
their horizons enough to be reached by the soul and its movements
at that particular time and in that particular culture. Giegerich
refers to these people as great people, artists and thinkers for
whom the soul that stirs in them has an event or fact character,
unpredictable. By "great people", Giegerich means:

> The great artist, the great thinker is consequently he or
> she who (not as person with his or her interior, his or her
> unconscious, but as *homo totus*) is reached by them or,
> the other way around, in whom, because he is reached and
> claimed by them, the great questions of the age ferment and
> can work themselves out. The great artist or thinker is no
> more than an alchemical vessel [Heidegger's the "there"—my
> insert] in which the great problems of the time are the prime
> matter undergoing their fermenting corruption, distillation,
> sublimation and of course articulation. And the real artifex
> of the work is ultimately the mercurial spirit stirring from
> within the *problems* of the age themselves. The great thinker
> and artist is thus he or she who can allow the *Mercurius* [the
> truth of our times—my insert] in the great questions of the
> age to do its stirring within himself or herself.[22]

These artists speak the truth of the time, and are indeed what
Jung would call mouthpieces of the age into which they were born,
just as he was when carving into the wall.

When Yeats writes in *The Second Coming*, for example:

> Turning and turning in the widening gyre
> The falcon cannot hear the falconer;
> Things fall apart; the centre cannot hold . . . ,

he is expressing the truth of the time in which he was born and as such is a great man. Like Jung the artist, he, too was auguring. In a few well-chosen poetic lines, he ushered in our post-modern world.

Jung's and Lockhart's subsequent amplifications of the carving as a document of the soul, suggest that the soul itself is emphasizing or highlighting the singular importance of inspiration, poetry, even madness, as those qualities of mind that will nourish the soul. These are the qualities of mind that soul herself is reaching out for. Their amplifications of Jung's carving, "after the fact", emerged as each man had to, at first, approach the completed carving as a "dead letter" which then quickened into a soul phenomenon, disclosing its meaning as the coming guest.

The methodology they each used is refined by Wolfgang Giegerich's art form of rising up to the level of soul and letting it have its say. In clearly specifying the coming guest as the psychological difference, i.e., the logical structure that lies behind and within our being-in-the-world today, Giegerich consistently cleaves to his conviction that "[a]ll it means [i.e., when the psychologist has risen up to the level of soul today—my insert] is to see "the guest" in the technological development and respect him as such"! No action is required of the human being beyond comprehending and respecting the coming guest. He amplifies the spirit of his conviction in another passage:

> We have to learn to *suffer* our hands to be empty, in the fullest sense of the word suffer. No image. No symbols. No meaning. No Gods: No religion.
> For is it not the empty hand, and the empty hand alone, that can be filled? As long as we cling to our religious traditions, we pretend to be in possession of something. We thereby prevent the advent of what can come, if at all, only as the free gift of the real world to

him who is ready to receive because he has nothing
whatsoever of his own accord, as the gift to him who
no longer, with a modesty that is disguised arrogance,
denounces our poverty as nihilism, but comprehends it
as the presence of the unknown future.[100]

Both Jung and Lockhart seem to have found their way to "the
empty hand", i.e., both were able to empty themselves out enough
to rise to level of soul, and receive its gift, as Giegerich advocates.
Both, however, were also able *to act on its hint in a work of art*: Jung
and his carving; Lockhart and his augury and book. Such reception
and enactment by the human being reflects another soul gesture,
one of incarnation, invoking symbolism of pregnancy and birth.[101]
Lockhart expressed the gift to him as this augury:

> In this sense the new age is not so much an age of
> consciousness as it will be an age of the poet—not the
> poet as noun, not the poet as career, but the *necessity*
> of poetry, the seeking by each one of us, a finding and
> drinking the waters and the milk of the Muses: poetry
> as verb, poetry as what we do . . . . [102]

When Jung was actually carving his high relief sculpture, i.e.,
performing his art, he, too was auguring, was making soul in the
sense of being pregnant with soul, ushering in its birth. He was
"doing his poetry":

> [W]hen he [Jung] gazed at the stone, the stone "spoke"
> to him. Jung "released" the images imprisoned there,
> brought them into view, into visibility. These are the
> experiences any sensitive sculptor would recognize. In
> this sense the artist is the means of liberation of images
> struggling for visibility not only in the psyche but in all
> matter as well![103]

After this long discussion, we have finally arrived at a
significant distinction in the methodologies or art forms in which
the psychologist or artist is acting as a mouthpiece for the reality
of the objective psyche as the background world-constituting

factor. This distinction will help us towards understanding a new definition of the artist that is springing from the necessities of our time in which the world is constituted as an expression of the logic of the psychological difference.

Wolfgang Giegerich describes the psychological difference as the difference between the human being (or ego) and "the soul" which are today dissociated from each other, thereby constituting the modern empirical world—a world of surface only, of literalism.[104] He describes his method or art form as a task, briefly, this way:

> [T]he psychological difference is inevitably no more than a *methodological* position that we may at times take, and to take which requires, as experience shows, some effort and poses quite a few difficulties.[105]
>
> [T]he task *vis-a-vis* the presenting complaint or prime matter of overcoming himself as empirical I (overcoming "the ego" standpoint within himself), in order to slowly work himself up into the standpoint of soul using the very material at hand as his guide as well as ladder.[106]

In practicing his method as an art form, the prime matter undergoes its own process of interiorization, taking the practitioner with it until, if she is fortunate, the totality of the dialectical opposition known as the psychological difference becomes explicit and the practitioner has "arrived" at the level of the living thinking that presently constitutes the modern world from behind and within its manifestations (the prime matter).

Here Giegerich's art form stops: comprehension and respect for the coming guest—a soul-making art form that temporarily, from the human side of the psychological difference, allows the human being to think out the autonomous thinking that constitutes our modern world. The practitioner then returns to empirical life, no doubt personally enriched but nothing else need follow (i.e., his method falls silent at this point) in the empirical realm that has any relevance for the world. In other words, the art form of psychology, *in its practice*, carries no necessary relevance for the world. The future, for Giegerich, is always only "let's cross that bridge when we come to it," i.e., when it has arrived and therefore is already behind us as the past (reflected).

We can see the limit to Giegerich's methodology most clearly in the following passage in which he offers his version of a cure to one of Jung's patients to whom Jung advised an "archetypal cure" to her neurosis through recognizing herself as a "Daughter of the Moon".

Giegerich correctly shows how such Jungian cures simply repeat the personal neurosis on a theoretical level, and how such mythological identities are completely out of reach for modern men and women. His, Giegerich's, cure therefore consists in:

> Why should she not be able, like everybody else, to find satisfaction, *contentedness*, in ordinary life? Perhaps by cultivating her garden, doing her daily duties, enjoying some good books and exhibitions, giving her neighbors a hand—perhaps also, and above all, by devoting herself to some useful task that would allow her to discover and employ *her* specific potential for being productive. Everybody surely can find some area where, some way how, to be productive. Why must she make such a fuss, unwittingly give herself airs as if she were perhaps a secret Queen in search of her missing crown insignia and the recognition due but denied to her? Why can't she be her ordinary self and find the way into the simplicity of life and of being human? Why can't she understand that there is nothing to be sought, nothing that would be somewhere else, be it in the future or in transcendence? Why can't she see that "this is it!"? It is this real life of hers that contains everything it needs within itself.[102]

We can see here that Giegerich's advice limits us to the life of mere Dasein. We simply go about our daily business and, as I said in my Preface, (as does Giegerich—see quote in Preface) the coming guest continues to unfold into actuality in its current "mechanical and soulless shape". Giegerich's art form of psychology as a discipline of *interiority*, is a methodology for addressing the upward soul gesture. The method enables the human practitioner to 'rise up' to the level of soul that lies behind and within the modern phenomena of our technological civilization and there think its dialectic, thus comprehending the soul life that gave rise to our modern world in the first place. The human practitioner then "returns to earth" no doubt personally enriched, where she then goes on with her life in some way that Giegerich's methodology can no longer advise or assist with beyond an admonition to "live long and prosper".[108]

So we must leave psychology as a discipline of interiority at this point and turn to another emerging art form and methodology, one that does indeed show *a way to live* that addresses the downward soul gesture, welcoming the coming guest in its thus redeemed form, rather than the presently appearing mechanical and soulless form that Giegerich so rightly notices.[109] [110]

In another context Russell Lockhart criticizes methods (such as psychology as a discipline of interiority—my comment) that only valorise experiences of (or participation with) the objective psyche as the sole goal of the work, on the basis that they miss the *fundamental* intention of Jung's psychology:

> The main purpose [of Jung's psychology—my insert] was the *incarnation of the realities of the Self.* The ego will not be transformed merely by experience of the imaginative psyche because the task is to bring the imaginative psyche into reality. If that equation is left suspended, if a route back into literal and material reality is not found, then nothing fundamental is ever accomplished.[111]

Wolfgang Giegerich has achieved a momentous advance in C. G. Jung's thought of what he, Jung, calls the Self. Giegerich has, for example, overcome the metaphysical (substantiating) tone of the word "Self", and resolved it into what we now know is in fact the psychological difference: not an entity at all within the human being, but the world-constituting logical structure of our modern world.[112]

Putting Lockhart's critique in the terms that Wolfgang Giegerich has developed, we can say that his (Lockhart's) criticism valorises, in its turn, any art form that promotes, or enables the logic of the psychological difference, the background "soul" structure that informs our world, to incarnate into materiality, this incarnation (pregnancy, birth), apparently being intended by soul itself, as Jung and Lockhart have augured respectively, and as Giegerich notes.[113] Such an art form, as yet unnamed, is described by Lockhart as "poetry as verb, poetry as what we do," or an "eros act", "enacting the dream's hint," etc.[114] These "poetic" acts, in contrast to Giegerich's art form are indeed of consequence for the individual and the world because they embody Eros, that power that is so stunningly absent in the world today:

> [W]ith the advent of the means of the means of extermination of all life as we know it, an unholy alliance has grown up between the rational intellect and this final power, this incarnation of Thanatos. With this supreme achievement of the patriarchal mind—which we might think of as burning the wings of eros with too much light—Eros must flee, must refuse to take up the battle in so much light, must seek, first, a nursing elsewhere.[115]

As my goddess and redeemer dream-visions show, when the human being can endure the psychological difference as it *incarnates* in him (as image in my case), he or she becomes pregnant with love, which is then born into materiality through the human's acting on the hint of the dream—an artistic or poetic act. These acts of love, based as they are on welcoming the coming guest, are in fact examples of the "little dream" that Jung speaks of to Sir Herbert Read which, when pooled with many other such "little dreams", give room for the birth of the coming guest, i.e., the psychological difference, i.e. its manifestation in the world as love—human love.[116]

THE NEW ART FORM: "POETRY AS WHAT WE DO"

Jung's little-discussed carving, his auguries that surround it, along with Lockhart's auguries throughout his book, *Psyche Speaks*, are hints of the emerging art form which Lockhart describes as "poetry as what we do"—an art form that is at the same time an act of love in the service of the soul's incarnation into the real world.

Although this new art form is still to be fully conceptualized and understood, let alone practised, there already are cultural products that act as further intuitions of its advent in our time. For example, there is a well-known widely defined form of literature called Magical Realism in which the process of the coming guest breaking through into actuality, through the human being, is explored *fictionally*.[117] Magical Realism explores the impact fictional reality (i.e., the reality of the coming guest) has on ordinary reality or, as C. S. Lewis puts it in reference to the books of Charles Williams, the effect of the "marvelous" *invading* the ordinary:

> [In Williams' novels]: We meet, on the one hand, very ordinary modern people who talk the slang of our own day and who live in the suburbs. On the other hand we also meet the supernatural—ghosts, magicians, and archetypal beasts. The first thing to grasp is that this not a mixture of two literary kinds. That's what some readers suspect and resent. They acknowledge on the one hand straight fiction: the classical novel, as we know it from Fielding to Goldsworthy. They acknowledge on the other the pure fantasy which creates a world of its own cut off in a kind of ringed

fence, from reality—books like Wind in the Willows . . .
and they complain that Williams is asking them to skip
to and fro from one to the other in the same work. But
Williams is really writing a third kind of book which
belongs to neither class and has a different value from
either. He is writing that sort of book in which we begin
by saying, "Let us suppose that this everyday world were
at some one point invaded by the marvelous".[118]

Lewis' description of an "invasion" of soul reality into empirical
reality is clearly not a birth image as much as an image of trauma.
The downward soul gesture of the soul is a *necessity*, and is thus
determinative.[119] The crucial factor in the *form* that the downward
soul gesture takes lies in the preparedness of the human being. As
Lockhart states:

> [M]adness must nourish psyche because in our
> enormous capacity to deny the imaginative reality that
> is psyche, to reserve reality only to the material world
> we call reality, that denied and rejected psyche will in
> fact become *matter* before our eyes. Who can deny the
> reality of psyche when one walks our streets today? It
> is visible, present, materialized in the behaviour and
> bodies and the voices we try not to see, try not to hear.
> Psyche has become real in this way because we fail in so
> many ways to grant psyche reality. [120]

In my previous books I explore Williams' work in more
detail, along with that of other authors.[121] The examples I give
there together show that an intuition is at work concerning the
incarnation of the coming guest and individuals are attempting to
imaginatively portray such an unheard-of process that is decidedly
new in history.

The incarnation of the coming guest is a process in which some
aspect of the objective psyche appears *as the human enactment* of
its purely fictional reality. The fact that some authors can sensitively
describe such processes imaginatively does not, however, mean that
the author has undergone the process *empirically*.

Can we find art forms today that express this unheard-of process in which the artist's enactment *in fact* gives birth to an aspect of the coming guest into actuality (rather than being intuited as seems to be the case in William's writing, for example)? Within the depth psychological tradition we need look no further than C. G. Jung's *The Red Book* in order to find a landmark example of an author who produced a form of literature that expresses the birth of a new reality (the coming guest) as it was happening through him as an *event*.[122] We still do not have a vocabulary for this new reality, so strange is it, but a key concept that Jung uses to describe the process of incarnation is "suspension". This concept alone should give us pause if we were inclined to rush its meaning into already-known categories of thought. In this process, the author is participating with the downward soul gesture *into* actuality (empirical reality) while rendering it as an art form at the same time.[123]

In 1934, Jung presented a seminar on Nietzsche's *Thus Spake Zarathustra*.[124] This appears to occur shortly after he emerged from his "confrontation with the unconscious".[125] With a little more distance from his wrenching experiences, he now began the task of giving form to his ordeal. In the seminars, Jung turns to the motif of suspension that implicitly appears in Nietzsche's book at the point where Zarathustra "buries the corpse in a hollow tree."[126] Jung's interpretation of this motif, as well as being an explication of what Nietzsche meant, clearly is also a hermeneutic exposition of his own recent ordeal. Yet it is so difficult to understand that, to date, no one seems to have subsequently explored or developed this thought any further in terms of the material of *The Red Book*.

Perhaps the most significant reason that Jung's discussion of "suspension" is so difficult to grasp is that it is almost impossible to language. Jung's years-long ordeal, as recorded in *The Red Book* was a sustained experience of suspension, as he encountered purely fictional figures *empirically*, i.e. with his empirical "I", rather than only his imaginal "I". If the images of fictional reality are first and foremost figures of speech, then we are approaching a profound mystery when we undergo such experiences with them, as Jung did:

> For the great mystery . . . is this: the appearance of a
> speaking figure, the very embodiment as it were in a

human-divine form of clear, articulated, play-related
and therefore enchanting, language—its appearance in
that deep primordial darkness where one expects only
animal muteness, wordless silence, or cries of pleasure
and pain. [127]

In my view Jung's ordeal was first and foremost an undergoing
of such an experience with language, in the sense that Heidegger
also means:

To undergo an experience with something [here
language] means that this something, which we reach
along the way in order to attain it, itself pertains to us,
meets and makes its appeal to us, in that it transforms
us into itself . . . . We speak and speak about language.
What we speak of, language, is always ahead of us. Our
speaking merely follows language constantly. Thus we
are continually lagging behind . . . Accordingly, when
we speak of language we remain entangled in a speaking
that is persistently inadequate. [128]

Thus, when Jung attempts to interpret the motif of suspension
in *Thus Spake Zarathustra*, springing from the soil of his own
experience, he is forced to draw amplificatory material from the
wide resources of his own scholarly background. For example he
speaks of suspension as:

- an aspect of crucifixion;
- the unconscious aspect of transfiguration;
- transformation being the fate of the body;
- transfiguration being the fate of the subtle body;
- preceding birth or creation;
- incubation of the subtle body;
- producing superior knowledge (like Odin's suspension and the
  art of writing);
- identification of the creator with what he is going to bring forth
  (see Heidegger quote above);
- torment in order to incarnate the unconscious contents;
- giving body to thoughts through "artistic" production;

- suspended ideas that express themselves as bodily symptoms;
- unconscious contents that "eat the sacrificed body" so that they can incarnate;
- ideas that take possession of the body;
- an initiatory process of "denying the body", inflicting terrible suffering so that a body can be produced in the mind. [129]

In reading the transcript of Jung's seminar, including the section on the motif of suspension, I am struck by the sheer force and flow of his extemporaneous language which seems to be a fountain or spring, flowing over with images drawn from scholarship but, at the same time, revivified with new meaning, as Jung appropriated (in the sense of hermeneutics) Nietzsche's work to his efforts of giving voice to his own violent ordeal of suspension.

For all Jung's efforts here in the Seminars and subsequently throughout his life, this process of suspension that characterized his ordeal as recorded in *The Red Book* remains a profound mystery and has received little attention by subsequent reviewers. [130]

I explore the concept of suspension in relation to the new art form in more detail in my recent book but I want here to give a taste of how "suspension" may be felt as the central concept that points to the new art form. [131]

In the following passage taken from *The Red Book*, Jung is confronted by a murdered child and a woman standing by, whose face is covered by a veil. To his horror, the woman demands that he eat the liver of the child. He does so:

> I kneel down on the stone, cut off a piece of the liver and put it in my mouth. My gorge rises—tears burst from my eyes—cold sweat covers my brow—a dull sweet taste of blood—I swallow with desperate efforts—it is impossible—once again and once again—I almost faint—it is done. The horror has been accomplished. [132]

We are not here merely reading an imaginative account of what it would be like to eat the liver of a murdered little girl. If it were, we could compare this graphic description with many other, equally compelling, and perhaps even fascinating horror stories such as those by Edgar Allen Poe, or Dante's journey through Inferno.

We are instead witnessing a first-hand account of the actual experience of the empirical Jung while in the realm of fantasy. Jung is not in the fantasy as an imaginal "I", as Dante was in *The Divine Comedy*, but as the empirical "I". *The Red Book* is analogous to reading a diary or a grotesque first-hand report of an actual act of cannibalism with the unheard-of twist that here, although Jung's reactions are empirical, the act is purely fictional! Moreover, this text suggests that, as well as Jung's "forcing his way" into fictional reality as an empirical ego, fictional reality itself was forcing itself "into" Jung. Empirical reality is here being penetrated by fictional reality.[133] It appears that *The Red Book* is a germinal art form that expresses this process of an interpenetration of fictional and empirical reality, which thus requires the man, Jung, to remain in a state of "suspension".

There is another compelling account of this process in which Jung participated.

He reports that on one occasion:

> . . . I tried to follow the same procedure, but it would not descend. I remained on the surface. Then I realized I had a conflict within myself about going down, but I could not make out what it was [the conflict then appeared to Jung as an image of two serpents fighting, one retired defeated and the fantasy then deepened] . . . I saw the snake approach me . . . the coils reached up to my heart. I realized as I struggled, that I had assumed the attitude of the Crucifixion. In the agony and the struggle, I sweated so profusely that the water flowed down on all sides of me . . . I felt my face had taken on the face of an animal of prey, a lion or a tiger. [134]

These reports come subsequent to the writing of *The Red Book* and as such are memories of Jung's experience yet they seem to me to be memories of the same process of the objective psyche entering empirical reality through the artist Jung.[135]

In my previous books, I have given other like examples from literature that seem to me to show a similar phenomenology—the author herself becoming the space or the "there" for an incursion of the objective psyche into empirical reality as she renders her experience in an art form.[136]

Lockhart's succinct phrase "poetry as what we do" beautifully conveys the meaning of the art form that welcomes the coming guest, the unknown future which is the background that always already informs our understanding within the modern world. I have elsewhere described this emerging future as an interpenetration of fictional reality and empirical reality.[137] Lockhart's phrase also suggests a *union* of these realities. The new art form therefore is also a doing, a way of living, ordinary life, although perhaps now with a new understanding of what "ordinary" means. The new art form must be consequential and based in responsible action in the real world thus uniting what has been sundered at least since the scientific revolution—the imagination and empirical reality.[138]

What could this look like, as a way of life—or should I now say—as a way of "art-life" since we have yet to find the language of such a reality?[139]

If we turn now to contemporary art, I think we may be able to see further strong manifestations of the new art form. It is no doubt true that:

> [C]ontemporary art is no longer one kind of art, nor does it have a limited set of shared qualities somewhat distinct from those of the art of past periods in the history of art yet fundamentally continuous with them.
>
> It does not presume inevitable historical development; it has no expectation that present confusion will eventually cohere into a style representative of this historical moment. Such art is multiple, internally differentiating, category-shifting, shape-changing, unpredictable (that is, diverse)—like contemporaneity itself.[140]

There are, however, at least two forms of contemporary art that seem to me to be representatives, or perhaps "harbingers" would be a better word, of the new art form that I am concerned with here i.e., performance art and installation art. In my view they are at least moving toward "a style representative of this historical moment", this "style" being the new world-configuring art form that is the coming guest or "poetry as what we do".[141]

There is a small video on *Youtube* that begins this way:

> Somewhere in a little town of Belgium
> On a square where nothing really happens
> We placed a button
> And waited for someone to push it . . . [142]

In the centre of the small town square is a pillar supporting a big red button. Dangling overhead is a sign: "Push to Add Drama". A passer-by does so and a drama erupts! Ambulances, accident victims, collisions between cars and people, fights, police and gangster shoot-outs all vie with one another while the local people look on.

Although it is easy to get absorbed in the dramatic action, it is quite instructive to also cast an eye on the locals who watched this advertisement for a TV station (as it turned out to be). Some were clearly shocked and then frightened. Others were nonplussed, uncertain, while still others became, in effect, the audience, enjoying the drama that exploded so unexpectedly into their lives "where nothing really happens". A purely staged event erupts into the empirical lives of ordinary people going about their business. It is striking to see how quickly some, if not most, understood what was happening and accepted it, even enjoying the "thrill" of it. This relatively quick adaptation to the incursion of drama into empirical life is reminiscent of earlier days when audiences at first fled the theatre as a cinematic train "rushed" towards them. Today we easily accept 3-D versions of these moving images, without thinking about the reality question at all. We merely enjoy the "thrill of the ride".

This kind of understanding is pre-reflective or on the way to becoming so. We simply comport ourselves in intelligent and appropriate ways within the new reality. For example, we remain seated, gasp with delight, and eat popcorn while a 3-D spear is hurled at our heads. So it is with this new performance art. The Belgian public (and by extrapolation, all of us) is beginning to move about intelligently and understandingly in a newly configuring world, and a correspondingly new way of being is emerging in the sense that Heidegger means: Dasein.[143]

It seems to me that such performance art is a concrete hint that the coming guest, that background of intelligibility that constitutes our modern world seeks incarnation into materiality. The reality of the objective psyche is penetrating empirical reality and these "category-shifting, shape-changing, unpredictable (that is, diverse)" art forms, *as informed by the background of intelligibility (the coming guest)*, are contributing to the contours of the unknown future.

The degree of ease with we are beginning to comport ourselves in this strange new reality is astonishing. I recently saw a documentary in which sports athletes are advertising . . . themselves! They are selling themselves as merchandise through an internet mechanism known as crowdsourcing (note that two words have become one in a linguistic contrivance that seeks to capture a new meaning "breaking in"). By soliciting small donations from thousands of anonymous donors, the athlete funds her way to the Olympics or some such event. In return, one athlete offered to carry the brand of the largest donor on her body as a tattoo (i.e. permanently). Such activity is also a variation of performance art in which an empirical life becomes a brand name.

Wolfgang Giegerich writes eloquently about such phenomena:

> The big sports events, watched by thousands or millions of people either live or on television, demonstrate to everyone who has eyes to see that man has in his essence been reduced to being a living advertising billboard . . . .
> [C]hampion sportsmen and sportswomen and the excitement they cause exist for the sake of advertising, advertising [a]s not just a negligible accessory to the all-important sports achievement and the excitement it causes. Furthermore, the fact that top soccer players are literally sold and bought by the various clubs should not be seen as an isolated phenomenon restricted to one limited area of life, sports. It is an isolated sign of the general truth about the essence of man, namely that he, too, has logically become merchandise, even if not empirically.[144]

Giegerich gives a good deal of psychological attention to the modern phenomenon of advertising. He comprehends the advertising industry's unstoppable tsunami-like reduction of the natural world to "empty form" or "external design" as:

> all-present and permeates almost all of modern life. Its task, too, is to translate all reality into the status of shadow and to bring this shadow character out into the open for everyone to see .... And then we would have to say that advertising celebrates what it touches for the (hidden) purpose of destroying (*logically* decomposing it, i.e., draining it of all inherent substantial meaning and dignity). The institution of advertising is a great mincing machine.[145]

From the point of view of psychology, such "performance art" is a soulless and mechanical manifestation of the unredeemed coming guest, appearing as such through the agency of those "suffering blind victims" who unconsciously identify with the life of the modern soul (the psychological difference) and act out its necessity.

It seems clear to me that various manifestations of these preliminary art and cultural forms, when produced by the conscious participation of "comprehending and feeling human beings", are also displaying the necessity of a unity between art form and way of being that together correspond with a new world, a new reality, as yet unknown—"poetry as what we do": the coming guest in *redeemed form*.[146]

AN EXAMPLE OF THE
NEW ART FORM

The upward soul gesture must begin with some manifestation of soul or a document of the soul (a document in which soul speaks about itself): "Myth or, for that matter, any book, any statement is a unity of an expression of the human subject and the self-expression of the soul."[147] Once reflected in the mind, it can undergo its own dialectical process of inwardization carrying the psychologist with it until its informing logical life is made explicit to and through the practitioner of the method. Thus, the psychologist rises up to *participation* with the current logical status of soul (the coming guest).[148]

The downward soul gesture, on the other hand, begins with the same soul manifestation. The artist then follows the hint of the unknown detail, that aspect of the soul phenomenon that has penetrated the psyche of the artist, leaving a resonant image or thought. She then enacts this hint into the real world. In so doing she participates in bringing some small aspect of the coming guest into manifestation in the real world in its *redeemed* form.[149]

And so, I begin with a dream:

> I am wandering the streets, alone. I find myself in a hall where some ritual is going on, conducted by an older man. The participants are each undergoing a ritual which seems perfunctory, i.e. just going through the motions. It has a Masonic-Christian feel to it. We are all sitting on our knees on carpet. When he sees me, he suddenly becomes interested, more alive, and asks me to go through the ritual which now comes alive. There is a

line on the floor. I am to touch my head on that line, i.e.
submit. I do so as he intones the ritual of confessions.
As I touch the floor with my head, he smiles and says
warmly you are forgiven, everything. Then he comes
over to me and crouches, whispering in my right ear
for some time. As I listen I hear the voice of the other,
a higher pitch, unearthly, i.e. the angel is speaking to
me though him. I have trouble understanding most of
it but the angel talks for some time. When finished I get
up but have trouble speaking. My right hand begins to
write automatically, I scribble "interlocutor". Afterwards
a younger man talks to me says and this is the first time
that ritual has gone for one hour, usually only minutes.

When I consider this memory text of the dream, two
movements start up in me. I desire to understand the dream, to
catch up, in consciousness, to the meaning of the dream (the logical
structure as which the dream, and I exist(s)). This movement is in
accord with the upward soul gesture. Simultaneously I remember
being *penetrated* by a certain aspect of the dream (the punctum),
which now leaves a resonant vibration in my soul. It is, in this case,
the image of the "interlocutor"—a vibration that I desire to follow
through enactment of this hint of the unknown future. This is a
moment of the downward soul gesture.[150]

In accord with my habitual valence towards "knowing", I decide
to follow the path of the upward soul gesture first. A number of
associations spontaneously gather around the dream, among
them the image of the street, a painting by Caravaggio, and an
astonishing psychological treatment of one of Jung's dreams by
Wolfgang Giegerich. Finally, a memory of a personal complex
emerges. Let's call it an authority or father complex.

Over the years I had quite a few dreams in which the context is
"the street". Among them, these two dreams, closely related to the
first:

> I am taken to the Cross where I am slowly nailed to
> it . . . . I feel the slow penetration of nails. The man
> slowly inserts one on my chest sideways and draws it
> through like a sewing needle. He does the same with

my left arm bicep muscle. The quality is of relentless, impassive certainty that this is what is happening. I am to endure it. It goes on for some time. There is no sadistic pleasure or horror. It is simply a doing to me! At last I look up and in the blue sky visions break through and I see sacred geometry. Then they are dragging me down the street, and they drop me there, leaving me on the street alone, no help. Abandoned casually as if nothing mattered to them about what happened. They just did their job and are now finished . . . .

and

I am alone, in a strange large city, perhaps to visit a friend . . . At some point I wander and get lost. I find my way into the city deep. In a bar, with strangers . . . I go sit at a table and the scene becomes or merges with a vast amphitheatre. A swell of people are flooding into it: devotees of a master. He has come. The tide of people rushing by me and he is there. I prostrate myself at his feet. He and I seem to be alone. He touches me and the kundalini energy rises again to the top of my head. Bliss! Apparently my friend has found me a bed to sleep in. I wake up later and I say I need to write down my experience with the master. Someone casually remarks that he died last night. I am shocked as I begin to discern the meaning of our encounter. As I walk down the street, sure enough I begin to feel his presence within as if I am being lifted by the seat of pants. Get going, he says, laughing . . . . Now there is a scene where I am planning with others a group of Catholic churches, no boundaries, open.

All three dreams seem to be emphasizing the *ordinariness* of the spiritual events taking place. They are taking place within the ordinariness of modern life, or *as* the within-ness (inwardness or soul) of ordinary modern life. This thought seems to be in accord with the dream fact of a worn-out ritual having a Masonic-Christian mood to it. The old man is the authority, the

"father-figure".¹⁵¹ In my submitting to the worn-out religious form
i.e. *to the loss* of that status of consciousness (logical form) that gives
rise to such initiatory rituals and external authorities, the ritual
"comes alive" as the new ritual in which submission, confession,
forgiveness, redemption from sin, and love are identical, springing
now from a new logical form in which the whole drama is the
inwardness of *'me' wandering the streets, alone, or 'me' on the street
alone, with no help, or 'me' alone, in a strange large city, wandering
and getting lost, in a bar, with strangers*. . . . The new form of ritual,
or initiation takes place as the inwardness of an ordinary lived life
and as the soul dimension of the wholly human as Giegerich shows
in a related discussion of the soul meaning of submission today (by
reference to Jung's dream of *Uriah*):

> The highest presence has . . . come down from the level
> of the gods and entered the human sphere with its
> suffering . . . . [One] fully bows to *his own* humanness
> and frailty . . . . *This* his submitting to his being without
> a God is his true humility. Man is here entirely for
> himself, but for himself not in the flat positivistic sense,
> inasmuch as now the whole former *relation between*
> man as upward-looking being *and* God as the goal of
> this upward-looking has been inwardized, integrated
> into the one *relatum*, man, and reoccurs as the inner
> dialectical logic of what being-human in the fullest
> sense of the word means . . . . [T]his submission is no
> longer to a positive Other, to God, and thus no longer
> religious. It is a logically negative submission, a self-
> contradictory self-relation. . . .¹⁵²

This "inner dialectical logic of what being-human means" is the
coming guest—the logical status of soul as "self", having already
been reached by soul historically, and thus implicitly informing the
structure of our modern consciousness, from "behind", as it were.
At the same time the coming guest is pulling us "from the future",
so that our consciousness may "catch up with" the status of soul
already reached, thus making it explicit:

> Although with Christianity the "Holy Ghost" *stage* of
> consciousness had been entered, it nevertheless took
> about fourteen centuries until man's implicitly already
> being in this stage was really caught with and the new
> truth had been integrated into the very structure of
> consciousness, its syntax or logical form.[153]

I experienced this pull "from the future" in the *punctum* of my
dream: the unearthly voice of the angel and the scribbled word,
"interlocutor".

Caravaggio shows Saint Matthew receiving the Word *directly*
from the angel, with his hand being guided by the angel's:

Such an image reveals a metaphysical understanding of soul.
The angel represents a divine other, separate from the human.
This is a form of consciousness that "substantiates" divinity as
a transcendent other, a form that, as my dream shows, is now
outmoded and lacking "life" (the Masonic-Christian form). My

dream, on the other hand, shows the dream-ego receiving the Word *as* the inwardness of an ordinary human discourse—the old man whispering in my ear, human to human. Here, the divine messenger is distinguishable but not separable from the human, occurring within the vehicle of language.[154] There is a contradictory unity here that is not present in the Caravaggio image, a unity that constitutes the (new) being-human.

Along with these dream facts, the word "interlocutor" seemed to me to offer a hint of what form the coming guest could here be "aiming at" in its downward soul gesture of manifesting in the real world. I decided to follow the hint.

Interlocution as speech or conversation *between* people seemed to carry some of the dream meaning with the angelic speech occurring "between" the two human speakers. I realized that I did not have much understanding at all about conversation. What are we doing when we have a conversation? I had no idea. Furthermore why do I get into a sudden, predictable flare of anger during conversations at certain points, when people speak to me in certain ways? I realized that conversation had always been important to me but, again, I had no idea why. I did not know what I was doing in a conversation or what a conversation between people was about.

It was time to find out!

I had been already engaged in an intense study of hermeneutics at the time, on the basis of a hint from yet another dream, so it wasn't long before I steered towards Gadamer's *Truth and Method* and dived into it.[155] I also began to pay attention to conversations in a new way. In particular I focussed on success and failure in conversation, and as well, disruptions to conversations that led, as I said before, to an angry flare-up on my part. My flare-ups were clearly linked to the kind of disruption that occurs when a participant in a conversation breaks off from attending to the subject matter and begins to focus on factors external to the conversation. Gadamer is well aware of this kind of disruption in his study of play as an analogy to the processes that occur in hermeneutical research:

> Play fulfils its purpose only if the player loses himself
> in play. Seriousness is not merely something that calls

> us away from play; rather, seriousness in playing is
> necessary to make the play wholly play. Someone who
> doesn't take the game seriously is a spoilsport. The mode
> of being of play does not allow the player to behave
> toward play as if toward an object . . . . The players are
> not the subjects of play; instead play merely reaches
> presentation (Darstellung) through the players.[156]

It became clear to me, then, that conversation requires losing oneself in it (i.e. overcoming the kind of consciousness based on subject-object relations), giving oneself over to the conversation in an attitude of openness that requires accepting "some things that are against me, even though no one else forces me to do so."[157]

I could suddenly account for my angry flare-ups. I wanted to surrender to the conversation, to the "subject-matter", completely, just as my dream of surrender suggested. This surrender is for the sake of understanding in the sense that:

> This understanding of the subject matter must take
> the form of language. It is not that the understanding
> is subsequently put into words; rather, the way
> understanding occurs—whether in the case of a text or
> a dialogue with another person who raises an issue with
> us—is the coming-into-language of the thing itself.[158]

In other words a successful conversation is one where the human participants surrender to the subject-matter in an attitude of openness to the other, such that a coming-into-being occurs, a self-presentation, as disclosed by language: My "angelic dream-being"! A failed conversation, on the other hand, is one in which the spoilsport breaks off from the dialogue, refusing to accept "some things that are against me", and moves back into the subject-object form of reflective consciousness that makes the subject matter, or the other human participant into an object: usually in the form of prejudice, pillory, or pathologizing. This refusal to surrender, which so violently disrupts the play of conversation, destroys the medium in which an appearance can occur within language. Depth fails to open up, interiority is shut down, and we are left on the surface, trapped in our positivist world, locked out from the depths of our own being.

I knew I was now getting closer to the mystery of the coming guest, that stage of consciousness already reached two thousand years ago, as which we (implicitly) exist today:

> With Christianity the "Holy Ghost" *stage* of consciousness has been entered . . . . [T]he story of the outpouring of the Holy Ghost upon the apostles . . . leads to a *linguistic miracle*, the speaking "with other tongues," a speaking that is understood by all "in our own tongue, wherein we were born." . . . the spirit expresses itself in something general or universal, communal, in language, in logos, in something that is interpersonal (or transpersonal) and public . . . other *tongues*, new general *logical forms* of consciousness, *within which* individual persons may have their place.[159]

By following the punctum of my dream, enacting its hint in the word "interlocutor", I was led to a great yet disturbing formulation concerning the fate of our times. The coming guest, as the already reached stage of consciousness (The Holy Ghost) is seeking, in a downward gesture of soul, to *appear* or self-disclose, in its present "form" of spirit (living thinking, logical life), as the inwardness or *depth* of language. Such appearance constitutes the *redeemed* form of the coming guest and as such requires human participation in its process of incarnation within language. The kind of required human participation is one in which the human interlocutors surrender to the language itself, remaining open to the other at all times. This kind of participation is essentially playful in that the habituated form of consciousness that we know as subject-object or Cartesian consciousness must be overcome in favour of a participatory form of consciousness that seeks understanding "as the coming-into-language of the thing itself"—the incarnation of soul as the "appearing" inwardness of language.

However, in our times, a *hardening* of the subject-object form of consciousness is occurring along with an incorrigible refusal to open to the other. The claim of the other is ignored or rejected:

In human relations the important thing is, as we have seen, to experience the Thou truly as a Thou—i.e., not to overlook his claim but to let him really say something to us. Here is where openness belongs. But ultimately this openness does not exist only for the person who speaks; rather, anyone who listens is fundamentally open. Without such openness to one another there is no genuine human bond.[160]

Yet the coming guest "wants" to incarnate in the human world and if it cannot do so in its redeemed form, then it will do so—and *is* doing so—in its mechanical and soulless form.[161] If we continue to maintain the *disjunction* between the human and divine through privileging our current form of consciousness, with its incorrigible need to know, then the coming guest will appear as a disruptive incursion, violent penetration into empirical life, as I have described in this book and elsewhere.

We know so little about surrender and fear it so much, but we can be taught:

FOREST
you are only lost
when you know
where you are going
surrender your certainty
death will show the way[162]

POSTSCRIPT

Shortly after completing a draft of this book, I purchased Wolfgang Giegerich's most recent book, *C. G. Jung on Christianity and on Hegel*, where I found a passage in which he succinctly draws out some further distinctions that clarify the intent and methodology of psychology.[163] In making these fine distinctions, Giegerich also provides us with a means to further differentiate the new art form from psychology (distinguishing what I call the downward soul gesture from the upward soul gesture—see my Dedication above).

In the chapter that contains the distinctions I am referring to, Giegerich examines Jung's uninformed and prejudicial attitude towards Hegel, an attitude that seems to downgrade the role of thinking in Jungian psychology in the sense of *"thinking* the real". This living thinking in effect involves an initiation of the consciousness of the practitioner, in contrast to the usual thinking *about* psychic facts, which involves only non-committal "knowledge of the facts". The difference between these two kinds of thinking is crucial to the question whether psychology is a psychology of the soul, in which the human being is initiated into soul reality, or whether it is simply another kind of ego-psychology in which psychic contents may be studied non-committedly by an observing ego which remains immune to the "objects of the study" via the logic of subject-object relations.

In order to make the distinction between the two kinds of thinking, Giegerich draws out a contrast between the method of active imagination as taught by Jung and Hegel's dialectic of thought, on the basis of what he calls self-movement (i.e., of image and thought). Although both methods require the steady gaze or close unwavering attention of the human "observer":

[t]he fundamental difference to the self-movement in active imagination is that *what* will happen in the imagination is determined by numerous unknown extraneous factors (the personality of the person practicing it, his memories, the contingencies of the person's history and present life conditions, etc.), whereas the self-movement of the concept simply unfolds sort of analytically (in the Kantian sense) the immanent moments of the concept itself, its "memory", its internal life . . . . The imagination may also follow laws, its own laws, but especially in the case of a modern ordinary person's deliberative active fantasizing—in contrast to great works of literature or art—it is highly contaminated by fortuitous subjective factors and in addition usually has a "synthetic character", narratively and additively passing from one image to the next . . . . Active imagination as the imagination in general, usually has no containing vessel and no hermetic seal. It can go on and on, and the image's self-movement can go off and away in all sorts of different directions and to new images. Not so the concept. It cannot go off. Being firmly enclosed in the retort, its self-movement is forced to go into itself.[164]

This is a stark contrast between methods indeed and serves to highlight Giegerich's allegiance to Hegel's thought and to his own practice of psychology as a discipline of (the logos of) soul. In this passage, and throughout Giegerich's works, there is a definite note of devaluation of image and the imagination in favour of thinking (not thinking *about*, but the autonomous logos of the soul—that status the soul has actually reached today in our time).[165] In order to *reach* the life of the soul today (which is in the *form* of thought, beyond image), the psychologist must re-enact in her own mind the process of sublation, as the "prime matter" (i.e., phenomenon under consideration), once reflected and therefore a property of the mind, undergoes its own dialectical negations towards making its immanent "moments" explicit to the mind of the psychologist. Of course this methodology demands cultivation of the mind to the degree that the psychologist can distinguish, in feeling, the difference between actively thinking as an ego *and* following or re-enacting the autonomous thinking of the phenomenon as it thinks itself out dialectically—no easy task!

Such a stark contrast deserves further scrutiny because, as it stands, Giegerich's global devaluation of the method of active imagination seems rather self-serving (i.e., serving his own interests as the pioneer of psychology as a discipline of interiority) and some important distinctions get lost in the process, even though he does here qualify his global attack on "the" method of active imagination by words such as "usually", "in general", "in the case of a modern ordinary person", etc. Giegerich's lumping together the great variety of methods of working with the imagination is for the purpose of negation—to spring off into uncharted (by psychology) territory i.e., the sphere of pure thinking. We can sense the negation at work in Giegerich's choice of words, such as "*contamination* [my italics] by fortuitous subjective factors"—a sure sign that one needs irrevocably to leave behind what subsequently must become a dangerous seductive factor needing defending against.[166] This posture of, shall we say, modesty, is an important aspect of Giegerich's programmatic refusal methodologically to consider the downward gesture of soul and thus to consider the new art form as having anything to do with soul movement and the future—this in spite of his many references to artists and their participation in the downward movement of soul into material reality (being *pulled* by the coming guest, etc).

We can see Giegerich's refusal at work most clearly in one of his many brilliant essays. In *Psychology as Anti-Philosophy: C. G. Jung*, Giegerich focusses on one of Jung's earliest active imaginations—his well-known and discussed encounter with a "forbidden thought" that he wrestled with for three nights before "letting go" and experiencing the image of the defilement of a cathedral . . . by God—i.e., God befouling his own house! Such a reported experience would be a clear case of active imagination as Jung subsequently developed it.[167]

This essay illustrates the difference between Giegerich's view of active imagination and the self-movement of the concept (see above), as well as his negation of *any* form of active imagination as being anything other than a movement running counter to the soul's movement today (i.e., towards absolute interiority). To explore all this we need first to start with Giegerich's *prime matter*, or phenomenon! He chooses a passage from *Memories, Dreams, Reflections* in which the old man Jung recounts his memory of the active imagination that he had when he was twelve years old.[168] It is *this* text that becomes the "dead letter" to which Giegerich turns his steady gaze, as psychologist. This text is now sealed off, as in a retort, and Giegerich makes no external interpretations. He stays within the text and follows the unfolding dialectic of its thought, its internal moments. In this effort Giegerich stays utterly true to his methodology and as a reader of his essay I found myself deeply enriched as I, too, began to think the thought of the phenomenon as it unfolded.

Jung's memory of God defecating on His own cathedral is structured by Jung in two parts: he first apprehends an autonomous thought breaking into his boyhood reveries, which brings him great anxiety. He wrestles against any further determination of the thought for three days until he gathers his courage enough to "let the thought come" and it did indeed burst through, but now in *image* form: the defilement of the cathedral brought about by God Himself!

By keeping his gaze focused entirely on the inner workings of this text, Giegerich shows that what appears on the surface as two separate thought events is in fact the dialectical unfolding of a single thought as it makes its implicit logic explicit. This self-movement of thought was however, prevented from unfolding *as thought* by "contaminating subjective factors" such as Jung's concerns for himself as well as for his own salvation and instead is held back on the level of thought as image. To be sure, Giegerich later on shows us how even this twist (Jung's resistance to thought in the *form* of thought) belongs to the soul's *telos* and in fact becomes the basis of Jung's later development of his structurally "neurotic" psychology.[169]

Giegerich's goal of showing how Jung's memory provides us with "the inner (ahistorical) principle" "of his entire intellectual life" in the essay does not concern us here.[170] The essay also shows us an exquisite example of Giegerich's methodology as practitioner of psychology as a discipline of interiority, where the psychologist follows the upward soul gesture into the realm of living thinking, beyond image and emotion, step by step into "the cold march of necessity in the thing itself . . .", and implicitly contrasts it with Jung's emerging method of active imagination "practiced" when he was only twelve years old, as reported by him, of course, near the end of his long life.

We can consider Jung's childhood encounter with the autonomous psyche as an eloquent representative of his method of active imagination since it bears many of the same structural elements of his later active imaginations, as described in *The Red Book*, and subsequently. Although this early example might be seen to contain what Giegerich calls "contamination of fortuitous subjective factors", there seems to me to be little else in Jung's report that conforms with Giegerich's description of how active imagination is supposed to work, i.e., "[a]ctive imagination as the imagination in general, usually has no containing vessel and no hermetic seal. It can go on and on, and the image's self-movement can go off and away in all sorts of different directions and to new images."[171]

None of Jung's active imaginations throughout his life, as reported to us, seem to me to have the phenomenology that Giegerich is here *negating*. It may be that his distinction between the "active imagination" of the ordinary modern person and that the "great artist or thinker" who produces "great works of literature or art" comes into play here (Jung clearly belonging to the latter group).[172] But Giegerich consistently addresses *all* of Jung's descriptions of his active imaginations only as texts that hold, within the imagery, an implicit thought that can be made explicit though re-enactment in the psychologist's mind. He has no other methodological use for such accounts or practices. Nothing in his writings seems to show any valence towards the practice of active imagination in terms of a downward soul gesture, i.e., the manifestation of the coming guest into material reality. The downward movement of the soul or autonomous psyche into material reality involves a penetration into empirical reality, a movement understood by Giegerich only as a *contamination* by fortuitous subjective factors—this being true only if one's valence is exclusively towards the upward soul gesture into the pure sphere of thought.

Giegerich clearly *recognizes* the downward soul gesture and maybe is the only analyst who gives a *psychological* account of the phenomenon of torture that accompanies so many of Jung's descriptions of his active imaginations during the time of *The Red Book*. But, again, Giegerich understands the "torture" only in terms of his own valence towards the upwards soul gesture and so we see his account of what I call Jung's *suspension*, "[t]he torment was absolutely necessary to really, and absolutely convincingly, install the new arena [of truth—my insert] in factual, bodily felt existence, in man as 'mere' *Dasein*."[173]

Giegerich here is talking about the logic of Jung's concept of the unconscious as being "within" empirical man. This interpretation of Jung's active imaginations during the time of *The Red Book* opens our eyes to the astonishing process in which the entire substance of the now logically obsolete metaphysical world was "swallowed" by Jung, fabricating in its turn the "inner" of empirical man.

Giegerich's interpretation of Jung's active imagination serves his purpose of demonstrating the neurotic structure of Jung's psychology *as a psychology of soul*. Giegerich wants to release this neurotic structure into its *truth*, rather than simply acting it out as so many practitioners of the art seem to do today. Releasing the structure of psychology into its truth apparently requires, however, as I have said, that Giegerich must negate the method of active imagination *in toto*.

Giegerich explicitly comprehends *The Red Book* as having an emphasis on the future, like Nietzsche's *Zarathustra* but in a way that "the two books are set completely apart". In contrast to Nietzsche who was working in the "sphere of absolute negativity", involving "the very definition of man and world", *The Red Book*:

- starts out from empirical man as a fixed given . . . ;
- [w]hen it talks of engendering and giving birth, etc., it means experiential processes in an always already presupposed positively existing man, the concrete individual as *Dasein*, literal man;
- the interiorization process . . . amounts to a reflection into the positivity of the human being as civil man and particular atomic individual;
- involves a shift from the universal (general) to the particular [and]

- a shift from the negativity of "spirit and truth" to positivity and literalism . . . and
- [a] prolonged, step-by-step process of sinking the *form* of thought into the *form* of the individual's . . . existential experience "in the flesh".[174]

These descriptions by Giegerich are profound insights into the phenomenology of Jung's active imaginations as recorded in *The Red Book* and show Giegerich's great insight into the direction of the soul gesture (downwards) that is revealed in *The Red Book*. Jung the *psychologist* called this new arena of truth the unconscious and built his psychology on this foundation, a foundation that Giegerich the psychologist has worked for decades to challenge so that psychology may be freed from the logical fetters that prevent us from exploring the truly philosophical problems of our time occurring as they do in the sphere of absolute negativity, "involving the very definition of man and the world".

In other words, while Giegerich recognizes and articulates the downward soul gesture in Jung's active imaginations, he evaluates such processes only in terms of his project to free the soul from "contaminations" so that psychology may "arrive" at its true nature as a psychology (of the logos of) the soul.[175]

As a result of Giegerich's evaluations and subsequent programmatic exclusion of any method of active imagination, however, the new art form inaugurated by Jung the *artist*, simply cannot be seen as a method that also serves soul in its *downward* gesture towards incarnating the coming guest in reality.[176]

My attempt here in this book is to show that the very same description of Jung's active imaginations in *The Red Book* also demonstrate the emergence of a new art form, one in which fictional reality (the autonomous psyche) penetrates empirical reality, with more or less logical violence, as a union of *telos* and contingency (those very contingencies that Giegerich downgrades to "contaminations").[177] The phenomena of Jung's "active imagination" experiences in *The Red Book*, do not present themselves in abstract conceptual terms. Theoretical concepts (the unconscious, the Self, god-image, anima, animus) belong to Jung's project as psychologist. The phenomena do not concern themselves with installing a hypostasized version of the objective psyche within Dasein—this is the *subsequent* labour of Jung the psychologist. All such theoretical talk is external to the phenomena. [178]

When I gaze into these texts they "speak" of the downward soul gesture and offer hints of a new art form that can adequately address the movement of the necessary incarnation of the coming guest into the real world in his *redeemed form,* if the process is participated by a "comprehending and feeling human being." I am convinced that C. G. Jung was such a human being and through him many aspects of the coming guest indeed incarnated, *The Red Book*, his high relief carving at Bollingen, and now as we can see his early childhood active imagination being outstanding examples. [179]

The artist of the new art form may gain courage from reading Jung's descriptions of the process of the soul's incarnation into actuality through his empirical reality enough to open herself to her own version of such processes (when and if they happen) and thus participate in the downward soul gesture, in effect becoming an agent of Love, as it enters material reality, gaining form yet remaining as spirit. This process requires *both* participation in the upward soul gesture:

> This Love is a real power, the ultimate objective reality. *But* it is only really present when as that which it is if there is a *real* "subjective awareness" of it in the sense of a mind having been "initiated" into it, that is to say, having itself, by going under, attained the logical form of . . . "the highest presence." [180]

And in the downward soul gesture:

> "Eros, the god which bringeth twain together in the service of life" . . . is a spirit that *desires*. And when this spirit penetrates consciousness, the individual is able to transcend the limitations of ego and to take part, not in ego's work, but in the "work of creation," that is, to participate in the birth of the future. [181]

INDEX

Index

A

active imagination 57, 58, 59, 61, 62, 63, 64, 99
actuality ix, 16, 35, 38, 40, 92
alêtheia xxiv
alien 1, 2, 3, 7, 17, 18
angel 49, 52
animal 41, 43
apocalyptic 73
archetypal 93
Aristotle xxi
art vii, xxi, 5, 6, 10, 23, 24, 27, 31, 32, 33, 34, 35, 36, 38, 40, 41, 42, 43, 44, 45, 46, 47, 57, 58, 59, 61, 62, 63, 64, 74, 75, 83, 84, 88, 90, 91, 93, 94, 98, 99
artist viii, ix, xv, xvii, xxi, xxii, xxiii, 5, 8, 10, 24, 28, 30, 31, 32, 33, 43, 48, 61, 63, 64, 76, 82, 83, 84, 92, 96, 97, 98, 99

B

background ix, xx, xxi, xxii, xxiii, 5, 6, 8, 13, 14, 18, 33, 36, 41, 44, 46, 81, 83, 84, 85
becoming 74
being 41, 43, 74
Being 78, 79, 81, 94
Being and Time 78, 79, 81

body 41, 42
Bollingen ix, 25, 26, 27, 28, 29, 30, 88

C

civilization xv, xvi, 7, 9, 10, 11, 13, 14, 18, 19, 20, 27, 36
coming guest viii, ix, xvi, xvii, 6, 8, 27, 31, 32, 38, 47, 59, 61, 63, 64, 78, 85, 90, 91, 98, 99
consciousness xxi, xxii, xxiii, 2, 5, 8, 9, 11, 13, 14, 17, 18, 22, 25, 27, 33, 49, 51, 52, 54, 55, 56, 57, 64, 74, 76, 78, 79, 80, 81, 84, 85, 94, 98
Consciousness Studies 73
contamination 59, 61
contingency xvi, xvii, 63, 96
conversation 21, 53, 54
crucifixion 41

D

Dante 42, 43
Dasein xix, 13, 14, 35, 45, 62, 63, 77, 85, 86, 94
defilement 59, 60
desire xvi
dissociation 15, 18, 21, 36
downward soul gesture 48, 49, 53, 64, 89, 90, 95, 96, 97

John C. Woodcock

dream xiii, xxv, 1, 2, 3, 4, 5, 6, 7, 19, 21,
    22, 23, 25, 37, 48, 49, 50, 52, 53,
    54, 55, 82
Dreyfus 78, 79, 81

E

ecstasy 4
empirical xxii, 14, 15, 17, 34, 40, 43,
    44, 45, 46, 74, 93
Empirical 43
empirical reality 43, 44, 61, 63, 64, 89
enact 58
enactment viii, 22, 27, 31, 33, 39, 49,
    61, 76
Ereignis xix, xx, xxi, 1, 78, 92
event ix, xiii, xix, xx, xxi, 10, 31, 40,
    45, 46, 83, 92

F

fantasy 43
fictional 40, 43, 93
fictional reality 40, 43, 93
form xiii, xvi, xvii, xxi, xxiii, xxiv,
    xxv, 3, 5, 6, 7, 8, 9, 10, 11, 17, 18,
    19, 21, 22, 23, 27, 32, 34, 35, 36,
    38, 40, 41, 42, 43, 44, 47, 83, 86,
    92, 93
future ix, xiii, xxi, xxii, xxiii, xxiv, 5,
    6, 7, 8, 10, 22, 23, 24, 25, 28, 33,
    34, 35, 44, 46, 73, 82, 83, 84

G

Gadamer xix, xx, 6, 9, 76, 78, 81, 82,
    83, 84, 85
gesture 22, 23, 24, 27, 33, 35, 36, 92
Giegerich xvii, xxi, xxii, xxiii, xxiv, 5,
    6, 7, 8, 9, 10, 15, 18, 19, 21, 23,
    27, 31, 32, 33, 34, 35, 36, 46, 75,
    77, 79, 80, 81, 82, 83, 84, 85, 86,
    87, 88, 91, 92, 94

guest ix, xvii, xxi, xxii, xxiii, xxiv, 6,
    7, 8, 10, 21, 23, 24, 27, 32, 37, 39,
    46, 77, 84

H

Hegel 57, 58, 75, 94, 95, 98, 99
Heidegger xvi, xix, xx, xxiii, 6, 11, 12,
    13, 14, 17, 18, 31, 41, 45, 77, 78,
    79, 81, 82, 84, 85, 86, 87, 92, 94
Herbert Read ix, xxi, 2, 24, 37
hermeneutics xix, 6, 9, 10, 42, 83
Hermes 92
historical xix, xx, xxi, xxiii, 4, 6, 8, 9,
    11, 18, 24, 29, 31, 44, 73, 86
history xix, 2, 4, 39, 44, 80, 81, 85,
    86, 93
horror 42

I

images 40, 42
imaginal 43
incarnate xvii, 4, 24, 28, 37, 41, 42
incarnation vii, ix, 6, 7, 10, 33, 36, 37,
    38, 39, 40
inception xx, xxi, xxv, 1
incursion 43, 45
individual xvi, xxi, xxii, 14, 37, 92
initiatory 42, 74
inner 74
intelligent xv, 45
intelligible 14
interiority 11, 35, 36, 54, 59, 60, 81, 90
interlocutor 49, 52, 53, 55
interpenetration 43
inwardization 48

J

Jung vii, ix, xvii, xxi, xxii, xxiii, xxiv,
    2, 4, 5, 6, 7, 9, 22, 23, 24, 25, 27,
    29, 30, 31, 32, 33, 35, 36, 37, 38,
    40, 41, 42, 43, 77, 78, 80, 81, 82,
    88, 91, 92, 93, 97

BIBLIOGRAPHY

Adler, G., & Jaffe, A. (Eds.). (1975). *C. G. Jung Letters* (Vols. 2 (1951-1961)). (R. F. Hull, Trans.) London: Routledge & Kegan Paul, Ltd.

Barfield, O. (1957). *Saving the Appearances: A Study in Idolatry*. London: Faber and Faber.

_____(1979). *History, Guilt, and Habit*. Irvington: Columbia University Press.

Berk van den. T. (2012). *Jung on Art: The Autonomy of the Creative Drive*. New York: Psychology Press.

Carmen, T. (2005). Authenticity. In H. L. Dreyfus, & M. A. Wrathall (Eds.), *A Companion to Heidegger*. Malden: Blackwell Publishing.

Dreyfus, H. L. (1995). *Being-in-the-World: A Commentary of Heidegger's Being and Time, Division 1*. Cambridge: The MIT Press.

Dreyfus, H. L., & Wrathall, M. A. (2005). Martin Heidegger: An Introduction to His Thought, Work, and Life. In H. L. Dreyfus, & M. A. Wrathall (Eds.), *A Companion to Heidegger*. Malden: Blackwell Publishing.

Edwards, J. C. (2005). The Thinging of the Thing: The Ethic of Conditionality in Heidegger's Later Work. In H. L. Dreyfus, & M. A. Wrathall (Eds.), *A Companion to Heidegger*. Malden: Blackwell Publishing.

Gadamer, H. G. (1977). *Philosophical Hermeneutics*. (L. E. David, Ed., & L. E. David, Trans.) Berkeley: University of California Press.

_____ (2013). *Truth and Method*. (J. Weinsheimer, & D. G. Marshall, Trans.) London: Bloomsbury Publishing.

Giegerich, W. (2001). *The Soul's Logical Life*. Frankfurt am Main: Peter Lang.

_____(2005). *The Neurosis of Psychology*. New Orleans: Spring Journal Books.

_____(2007). Psychology as Anti-Philosophy: C. G. Jung. (N. Cater, Ed.) *Spring: A Journal of Archetype and Culture, 77*(Philosophy and Psychology), 11-52.

_____(2007). *Technology and the Soul*. New Orleans: Spring Journal Publications.

_____(2008). *Soul Violence*. New Orleans: Spring Journal Books.

_____(2010). Liber Novis, that is, The New Bible. A First Analysis of C. G. Jung's Red Book. (N. Cater, Ed.) *Spring: A Journal of Archetype and Culture, 83*(Minding the Animal Psyche), 361-412.

_____(2012). *What is Soul*. New Orleans: Spring Journal Books.

_____(2013). *Neurosis: The Logic of a Metaphysical Illness*. New Orleans: Spring Journal Books.

Heidegger, M. (1982). *On the Way to Language*. (P. D. Hertz, Trans.) San Francisco: Harper.

Jaffe, A. (Ed.). (1979). *C. G. Jung: Word and Image*. Princeton, Princeton University Press.

Jung, C. G. (1963). *Memories, Dreams, Reflections*. (A. Jaffe, Ed., C. Winston, & R. Winston, Trans.) New York: Random House.

_____(1975). *C. G. Jung Letters* (Vols. 2 (1951-1960)). (G. A. Adler, Ed., & R. F. Hull, Trans.) London, Routledge and Kegan Paul.

_____(1988). *Nietzsche's Zarathustra: Notes of the Seminar Given in 1934-1939.* (J. L. Jarrett, Trans.) Princeton, Princeton UNiversity Press.

_____(1989). *Analytical Psychology: Notes of the Seminar Given in 1925.* (W. McGuire, Trans.) Princeton: Princeton University Press.

_____(2009). *The Red Book.* (S. Shamdasani, Ed.) New York, Norton.

Kerenyi, K. (1990). *Hermes: Guide of Souls.* Dallas: Spring Journal Books.

Lewis, C. S. (n.d.). C. S. Lewis Lectures on the Novels of Charles Williams. Retrieved 11 29, 2012, from https://www.youtube.com/watch?v=Z5w134gYz04.

Lockhart, R. A. (1987). *Psyche Speaks: A Jungian Approach to Self and World.* Wilmette: Chiron.

Marlan, S. (2006). From the Black Sun to the Philosopher's Stone. (N. Cater, Ed.) *Spring, 74*(Alchemy), 1-30.

Mogenson, G. (1994). "The Collective Unconscious and the Leontocephalus: A Rejoinder to Noll": Letter to the Editor. *Spring: A Journal of Archetype and Culture, 56.*

Noll, R. (1992). Jung the Leontocephalus. *Spring Journal: A Journal of Archetype and Culture, 53.*

Polt, R. (2005). Ereignis. In H. L. Dreyfus, & M. A. Wrathall (Eds.), *A Companion to Heidegger.* Malden: Blackwell Publishing.

Smith, T. (2012). *Contemporary Art: World Currents.* London: Laurence King Publishing.

Woodcock, J. C. (2009). *Transformation of the World.* Bloomington: iUniverse.

John C. Woodcock

_____ (2011). *The Imperative*. Bloomington: iUniverse.

_____ (2012). *Animal Soul*. Bloomington: iUniverse.

_____ (2013). *Making New Worlds: The Way of the Artist*. Bloomington: iUniverse.

_____ (2013). *Manifesting Possible Futures: Towards a New Genre of Literature*. Bloomington: iUniverse.

_____ (2013). *Overcoming Solidity: World Crisis and the New Nature*. Bloomington: iUniverse.

_____ (2013). *Ur-image*. Bloomington: iUniverse.

Wrathall, M. A. (2005). Unconcealment. In H. L. Dreyfus, & M. A. Wrathall (Eds.), *A Companion to Heidegger*. Malden: Blackwell Publishing.

ABOUT THE AUTHOR

John C. Woodcock holds a doctorate in Consciousness Studies (1999). His thesis articulates the process and outcome of a spiritual ordeal that lasted twenty years. At first it seemed to John that he was undergoing a purely personal psychological crisis but over time, with assistance from his various mentors, he discovered that he was also participating in the historical process of a transformation of the soul as reflected in the enormous changes occurring in our culture, often referred to as apocalyptic. During this difficult period of John's life, he wrote two books: *Living in Uncertainty Living with Spirit* and *Making of a Man*. Both books are now expanded into second editions (2012).

Over time John began to discern soul movement comprising hints of the unknown future, from within our present apocalyptic upheavals, John's next three books, *The Coming Guest, The*

Imperative, and *Hearing Voices*, explore this idea more fully by describing the initiatory process and outcome of a human being's becoming a vehicle for the expression of the unknown future, through the medium of his or her art. John's next two books, *Animal Soul*, and *Manifesting Possible Futures*, establish a firm theoretical ground for the claim that the soul is urging us towards the development of new inner capacities that together can discern and artistically render hints of possible futures through participation and resonance. His book, *Overcoming Solidity*, continues this exploration of transformation of "worlds". Its focus is on our current structure of consciousness and its correlative world which we call empirical reality. He shows how the development of capacities necessary to discern hints of possible futures involves a kind of violence, due to the "solidity" of modern-day consciousness. His latest book, *Making New Worlds*, begins the work of articulating the art form that is emerging in response the soul's intention to incarnate in the real world.

John currently lives with his wife Anita in Sydney, where he teaches, writes, and consults with others concerning their own journey through the present "apocalypse of the interior", as it has been called, in his capacity as a practicing Jungian therapist. John and Anita also work with couples in a therapeutic setting.

He may be contacted at *jwoodcock@lighthousedownunder.com*

END NOTES

1   Giegerich, W. (2008). *Soul Violence*. New Orleans. Spring Journal Books. P. 298.

See also his book, Giegerich, W. (2001). *The Soul's Logical Life: Towards a Rigorous Notion of Psychology*. Frankfurt am Main. Peter Lang.

We can get a sense of Giegerich's art form and the difficulties involved in its practice from the following quote. Giegerich likens the modern task of psychology to "discerning the spirits" or "trying the spirits" to test whether they are "of God". By this biblical analogy, he is suggesting a method that can discern psychological "'truth': the living truth in which and out of which a people *psychologically* in fact lives." This method requires:

. . . our coming forward with a personal judgement, our taking a stand, hopefully on the basis of a certain psychological sophistication, a refined sensitivity, a well-developed feeling-function in things psychological, an "intelligence du coeur" and above all a differentiated mind—a mind that has the distinction between the truly archetypal and the phony (the nostalgic, the sentimental, imitations, simulation, etc.) as categories at its disposal. [See Giegerich, W. (2014). *C. G. Jung on Christianity and on Hegel*. New Orleans. Spring Journal Books. P. 75.]

Can this method withstand the usual "post-modern" accusations of "prove it," or "this is only your opinion" etc? Of course it can! Giegerich's method has its objectivity in the sense that two practitioners of the art can agree on the "truly psychological" in much the same way as wine connoisseurs agree on the subtle objective qualities of a rare wine. Gadamer's relevant essay: "The Question of Truth as It Emerges in the Experience of Art" in *Truth and Method* explores the history of *Bildung* (cultivation of the human being). See Bibliography.

2   Lockhart, R. A. (1987). *Psyche Speaks: A Jungian Approach to Self and World.* Wilmette. Chiron.

3   Woodcock, J. C. (2012). *Animal Soul.* Bloomington. IUniverse.

4   See n. 122 for Heidegger's notion of an *event.*

5   Such memory has to be considered, strange as it sounds, as "memory of the future". By this I do not mean any knowledge of the future in its positive-factual reality. Rather, we can think of it in terms of initiation where the soul background of the world (the unknown future, or the coming guest) imprints itself, as image or thought, in the "artist" who then enacts its hints in the real world so that it *becomes* her/our (explicit) future. Lockhart puts it this way, ". . . the secret connection with the Self is revealed through *enactment* of the ethical obligations learned and remembered in secret consort with the Self." Op. cit. P. 15. Such "imprinting" is the initiatory meaning of scarification.

6   The push of 20ᵗʰ C. philosophy was towards articulating the being that is logically prior to reflections about being. Put another way, after centuries of a definition of humans as isolated subjectivities forever separated from a world bereft of any subjectivity or consciousness, we seem to be moving towards a definition of the human being as a 'clearing' or the 'there' where mind and world appear in the first place, pre-reflectively. I use the word 'participation' after Owen Barfield to point to the phenomenology of that 'place' where human and world *appear.*

7   Lockhart, R. A. *Psyche Speaks: A Jungian Approach to Self and World.* Op. cit. P. 48.

8   Yeats, W. B. *The Second Coming.*

9   Gadamer, H-G. (2013). *Truth and Method* (Bloomsbury Revelations). Bloomsbury Publishing. Kindle Edition. Location 2128.

10   See: Friedrich Nietzsche. (1997). *Daybreak: Thoughts on the Prejudices of Morality* (Cambridge Texts in the History of Philosophy). Kindle Edition:

In comparison with the mode of life of whole millennia we present-day men live in a very immoral age: the power of custom is astonishingly enfeebled and the sense of morality so rarefied and lofty it may be described as having more or less evaporated. (Kindle Locations 320-321)

[11] Dasein is that being that seeks to understand being, for whom being is an issue. Heidegger's great contribution to 20th C. philosophy is to draw our attention to and articulate for the first time in modernity, our *pre-reflective* being i.e., the way in which we comport ourselves intelligently and understandingly in the world, prior to any reflection on what we are doing. This understanding is given to us. It is always "behind us" and much of his philosophy is oriented to philosophical description of the being that lies behind beings such as ourselves. One way to put this is to ask: how can we account for presence itself? How do things show up in the first place? See: Wrathall, M. A. "Unconcealment" in *A Companion to Heidegger* (Blackwell Companions to Philosophy, Vol. 29) (Kindle Locations 6891-6904). Kindle Edition.

[12] Giegerich, W. (2012). *What is Soul?* New Orleans. Spring Journal Books. P.30.

[13] Ibid. P. 325.

[14] Giegerich, W. *The Soul Always Thinks.* Op. cit. P. 508 n. Here is the full quote:

In matters of the soul process it does not matter very much whether we agree or not. It will happen anyway . . . . However, depending on whether the guest comes *vocatus* or whether he comes *non vocatus* there is a great difference in *how* his arrival will happen, that is to say, what it will mean for us and how it will affect us. Seneca wrote, and Jung would certainly have agreed: *Ducunt volentem fata, nolentem trahunt,* "If you are willing, fate will guide you, if you are not, it will drag you" (*Epistulae morales*, 107, 11). Similarly, Thomas Mann said (in *Joseph and his Brothers*), "If you can do it, you will do it. If you cannot, it will be done to you." That's the difference. And it makes all the difference *for us*, the difference between "suffering blind victim" and "comprehending and feeling human being." But it makes also an essential difference for the arriving new reality. If we resist, this reality will be mechanical and soulless. If we see the guest in it, *our* guest, indeed our deepest self, it can appear in redeemed form.

15   Jung, C. G. (ed. G. A. Adler, & tr. R. F. Hull) (1975). *C. G. Jung Letters (Vols. 2 (1951-1960).* London: Routledge and Kegan Paul. P. 591. For full quote see Chapter: "Jung's Hidden Legacy As Artist".

16   There appears to be a paradox here. How, in a time of soullessness, *can* we serve soul (the coming guest)? From the point of view of soul, the modern world with its logic of externality is simply another moment of soul-life—a moment in which soul ejected itself out of its inwardness to a stance of external reflection. But this external standpoint is still "within" soul, since we can never "get out" of soul. Our empirical lives, which are now in a mode of consciousness called "external reflection", are still within soul—this "paradoxical" totality being another formulation of Wolfgang Giegerich's critical notion of the psychological difference as which we exist today. See Index for references to the psychological difference and Endnotes for citations.

17   For a more detailed examination of the redeemed form of the coming guest see my Chapters: "Our Redeemer" and "An Example of the New Art Form".

18   Gadamer, H-G., Linge, D. E. (tr./ed.) (1977). *Philosophical Hermeneutics.* Berkeley. University of California Press. P. xxviii.

19   Polt, R. "Ereignis"in *A Companion to Heidegger* (Blackwell Companions to Philosophy, Vol. 29) (Kindle Locations 6891-6904). Kindle Edition.

20   Ibid. (Kindle Location 7004-7009). Kindle Edition.

21   Gadamer, H-G., Linge, D. E. (tr./ed.). *Philosophical Hermeneutics.* Op. cit. P. liv.

22   Lockhart, R. (1987). *Psyche Speaks.* Op. cit. P. 25. I discuss the "violence" of this punctum in my book, Woodcock, J. C. (2013). *Overcoming Solidity: World Crisis and the New Nature.* Bloomington. iUniverse.

23   Dreyfus, H. L. (1995). *Being-in-the-World: A Commentary of Heidegger's Being and Time, Division 1.* Cambridge. The MIT Press. See Chapter 10: "Affectedness".

24   The term, "the 'there'" is from Heidegger: "Ereignis . . . takes place only when a place is established, not in events within an established place." Polt, R. "Ereignis". Op. cit. Kindle Locations 6914-6915.

Although Ereignis is a very complex concept, it does seem to point to the human being as being the "space" where an inception from of the objective psyche may occur. See also Dreyfus, H. L. (1995). *Being-in-the-World: A Commentary of Heidegger's Being and Time, Division 1.* Op. cit. See Chapter 9: "The Three-Fold Structure of Being-In".

25   We of course always live in the same world but it is the same world as constituted differently (form) throughout the ages. Today, we in fact live in (the logic of) two worlds, one modern, one obsolete. In our subjective psyches we inhabit a metaphysical world (the logic of substantiality) while as Daseins we comport ourselves quite understandingly within the logic of our technological civilization, while remaining quite unconscious of the *being* of that world in which we so comport ourselves. This is an expression of Wolfgang Giegerich's notion of the psychological difference (see Index for references). When I speak of the objective psyche "breaking through into the consciousness of an individual", I am talking about the background intelligibility that produces the *form* of our modern technological civilization within which we live, in our conduct, understandingly. Such an intrusion into the subjective psyche threatens or challenges its stability, or its constituting logic of substantiality (metaphysics) and the individual can experience "the end of the world". This means that the individual experiences, with more or less violence, a collision between her self-definition (as constituted by the logic of metaphysics—e. g. I am a solid self, the world is filled with Meaning, etc) *and* her definition, as expressed in her very comportment through life—e. g. "I now live in an age of mythlessness, there is no centre, no absolute guidance from the outside, I live in the knowledge that my identity is now digitalized, fluid, etc.)". There are now more and more movie scripts being produced that explore this theme of fluid identity ("I can be anybody I want", etc.), usually set in a context of scams or hustles, and of course the entire acting industry is an exercise in fluid identity. See Chapter: "Our Redeemer" for two examples of such "world-altering" intrusions into my subjective consciousness.

26   Giegerich, W. *What is Soul?* Op. cit. P. 187.

27   Giegerich, W. *The Soul Always Thinks.* Op. cit. P. 509 n. As we will see later, I dispute Giegerich's claim that "all the soul . . . needs is

needs is to have a real echo, a resonance in ourselves, to be seen, acknowledged, and appreciated for what it is." The soul also needs (i.e. its necessity and determinative power) to incarnate into actuality and does so through the human being who may be its unwilling victim or its participating servant as "comprehending and feeling heart".

[28] Jung, C. G. (ed. G. A. Adler, & tr. R. F. Hull). *C. G. Jung Letters (Vols. 2 (1951-1960). Op. cit. P. 591.*

[29] See Lockhart's discussion of this letter in *Psyche Speaks.* Op. cit. P. 51 ff.

[30] Giegerich, W. *The Soul Always Thinks.* Op. cit. P. 512.

[31] Ibid. Pp. 509, 516, 526 (n. 26).

[32] As translated by Wolfgang Giegerich. See *What is Soul?* Op. cit. P.187.

[33] Ibid.

[34] Giegerich, W. *Soul Violence.* Op. cit. P. 81. In the same passage Giegerich names the new way of seeing life as a whole, *psychology!* I left the term out here because to understand his meaning requires too much discussion for this small space but suffice to say that he does not mean psychology as a discipline among other disciplines, such as science, biology, history, religion, etc., each having its own content which the "observer" can know! Psychology (the logic of the psychological difference) is the sublation of all these disciplines which are all rooted in the logic of subject-object relations.

[35] See n. 24 for "the 'there'".

[36] Giegerich, W. *What is Soul?* Op. cit. P. 188.

[37] The following brief description of Wolfgang Giegerich's original contribution to depth psychology may be found at http://www.ispdi.org:

> In the course of a prolific writing career that commenced in the early 1970's and which now spans four decades, Giegerich has made a most incisive contribution to a truly psychological psychology . . . . The depth psychology that began with Freud, Adler, and Jung was itself but a late expression of the history of consciousness, the history of the soul. Passing through many stages and statuses on its way to becoming conscious of itself—stages such as the shamanic/ritualistic, the mythological, the religious, the metaphysical, and so on—consciousness only "came home to itself" very recently in such

simultaneously phenomenal and theoretical expressions as the philosophies of the subject, medial modernity, and contemporary depth psychology. And to this list there may now be added psychology as the discipline of interiority.

[38] For a thorough discussion of how we understandingly conduct our lives in the world, see Dreyfus, H. L. *Being-in-the-World: A Commentary of Heidegger's Being and Time, Division 1.* Op. cit. Chapter: "Worldliness".

[39] To understand how we exist today "remaining in the past" while at the same time comporting ourselves as modern individuals, we need Wolfgang Giegerich's pivotal concept of the psychological difference in which he makes the crucial distinction between the psychic and the psychological (objective psyche). The "psychic" is the "stored" treasure house of history (former states of consciousness) that may be found within while the soul/objective psyche is the background intelligibility that informs our actual comportment in life today. For a comprehensive study of the psychological difference as psychic/soul difference, see: Giegerich, W. (2006).*The Neurosis of Psychology.* New Orleans. Spring Journal Books. Pp. 103-117.

[40] Giegerich, W. *What is Soul?* Op. cit. P.188.

[41] Jaffe, A. (ed.) (1979). *C. G. Jung: Word and Image.* Princeton. Princeton University Press. P. 136.

[42] Giegerich, W. *The Soul Always Thinks.* Op. cit. P. 508n.

[43] Ibid. P. 509 n.

[44] Giegerich, W. *What is Soul?* Op. cit. P. 188. The "life-time's work" has begun with my writing ten books, all self-published through iUniverse.com.

[45] See my autobiographical account of my dream-visions: Woodcock, J. C. (2011). *The Imperative.* Bloomington. iUniverse.

[46] An account of my twenty-year long ordeal may be found in my book: Woodcock, J. C. *The Imperative.* Op. cit. To gain some distance from the at-times overwhelming material, I use the name of "David" in my autobiographical account.

[47] Gadamer, H-G., Linge, D. E. (tr./ed.). *Philosophical Hermeneutics.* Op. cit. P. xxv.

48 Jung, C. G. (ed. Jarrett, J. L.) (1988). *Nietzsche's Zarathustra: Notes of the Seminar Given in 1934-1939*. Princeton. Princeton University Press. Pp. 184 ff.

49 See my latest book: Woodcock, J. C. (2013). *Making New Worlds: The Way of the Artist*. Bloomington. iUniverse. Chapter: "The Violent Character of the New 'Art Form'".

50 I first met Wolfgang Giegerich through correspondence in 1997, when I was completing my doctoral program. At the time he and James Hillman were engaged in a theoretical dispute which led to a further differentiation within depth psychology: Hillman had pioneered Archetypal Psychology and Giegerich went on to establish "Psychology as a Discipline of Interiority", or PDI. My book *Animal Soul* (see Bibliography) is my attempt to explore the subtle theoretical differences between Hillman and Giegerich in regards to one concept, the *anima mundi*! Giegerich's books were later published by *Spring Journal* and I immersed myself in them. I contacted him again in 2008 and a rich correspondence followed in which he generously answered any question I had regarding PDI. As I slowly began to focus on my own interests (soul and the future), we parted ways. This book is my attempt to understand the (soul) necessity of parting ways.

51 My engagement with any scholarly research almost always begins with a dream and my "enacting the hint of the dream". So it was with Heidegger and Gadamer. For a full discussion of this unusual approach to knowledge, see my book, *Making New Worlds: The Way of the Artist*. Op. cit.

52 In the sense that Gadamer means:

It is imagination [Phantasie] that is the decisive function of the scholar. Imagination naturally has a hermeneutical function and serves the sense for what is questionable. It serves the ability to expose real, productive questions, something in which, generally speaking, only he who masters all the methods of his science succeeds. (Gadamer, H-G. *Philosophical Hermeneutics*. Op. cit. P. 12.)

53 *The International Society for Psychology as the Discipline of Interiority*: http://www.ispdi.org. The theoretical basis of my dispute with ISPDI is a hermeneutical one. In studying the work of Wolfgang Giegerich—work that is the sole authority for PDI—are we reaching

for a canonical (reproductive) understanding, or as Giegerich himself writes, a hermeneutical one in the sense that Gadamer means too:

> The soul leaves the works as positivities that it produced behind . . . and these works, the expression of a former "spark," can be the inspiration for a new "spark" in persons of a new generation. "New" in "new spark" does not here mean a new occurrence or event (i.e. repetition) of the same spark that once produced the work, but truly new, different: a new meaning. (Giegerich, W. *What is Soul?* Op. cit. P. 72.)

> [A]n author does not need to know the real meaning of what he has written; and hence the interpreter can, and must, often understand more than he. But this is of fundamental importance. Not just occasionally but always, the meaning of a text goes beyond its author. That is why understanding is not merely a reproductive but always a productive activity as well. Perhaps it is not correct to refer to this productive element in understanding as "better understanding." . . . It is enough to say that we understand in a different way, if we understand at all. (Gadamer, H. G. *Truth and Method.* Op. cit. P. 307.)

54 See in particular Giegerich's book, *What is Soul?*. Op. cit.

55 Apart from the differences in our hermeneutics when reading the texts of Wolfgang Giegerich, another difference arose in which, during my efforts to address the question of the soul and the always unknown future, I was most often charged with attempting to anticipate the future in its positive-factual aspect. This book, then, is my attempt to clarify that misunderstanding. I am exploring that art form which addresses the soul background of our modern world, a background that is always already behind us (past), yet which nonetheless pulls on the artist from the future as "the coming guest", as I describe in these pages, i.e., the logic of the concept *hysteron proteron* or uroboric logic.

56 This rejection of my proposals seemed to fly in the face of Giegerich's many descriptions of the artist's participation in the soul's manifestation in the world (as negative reality, to be sure). I later concluded that the rejection was programmatic, rather than argued.

57 See n. 52.

58 See n. 14.

59   Owen Barfield discusses this possibility in relation to art and the imagination now freed from "imitating nature":

> Imagination is not, as some poets have thought, simply synonymous with good. It may be either good or evil. As long as art remained primarily mimetic, the evil which imagination could do was limited by nature . . . [b]ut . . . when the fact of the directionally creator relation is beginning to break through into consciousness, both the good and evil latent in the working of imagination begin to appear unlimited. . . . we could very well move forward into a chaotically empty or fantastically hideous world . . . .
>
> We should remember this, when appraising the aberrations of the formally representational arts . . . . in so far as they are genuine, they are genuine because the artist has in some way experienced the world he represents. And in so far as they are appreciated, they are appreciated by those who themselves are willing to make a move towards seeing the world in that way and, ultimately therefore, seeing that kind of world. We should remember this, when we see pictures of a dog with six legs emerging from a vegetable marrow or a woman with a motor-bicycle substituted for her left breast. [Barfield, O. (1957). *Saving the Appearances: A Study in Idolatry.* London. Faber and Faber. Pp. 145-6.]

60   The coming guest *as* pulling the artist from the unknown future and *as* the background logic that always already constitutes our modern world can only be understood as an unfoldment of uroboric logic or *hysteron proteron*.

61   Giegerich, W. *The Soul Always Thinks.* Op. cit. P. 509n.

62   Giegerich, W. Ibid. Pp. 512, 516, 526 (n. 26).

63   Giegerich, W. *Soul Violence.* Op. cit. P. 81.

64   Gadamer, H-G., Linge, D. E. (tr./ed.). *Philosophical Hermeneutics.* Op. cit. Pp. 3 ff.

65   Dreyfus gives an excellent account of the historicity of "worlds": "[H]istory means the series of total worlds that result from a struggle of interpretations as to the meaning of being." See: Dreyfus, H. (2005). "Heidegger's Ontology of Art" in *A Companion to Heidegger* (Blackwell Companions to Philosophy, Vol. 29) (Kindle Location 7552). Kindle Edition.

66   See Giegerich, W. "The Alchemy of History" in *Soul Violence.* Op. cit.

67 Psychology throughout here means PDI as pioneered by Wolfgang Giegerich: Psychology as a Discipline of Interiority. By claiming that the coming guest is psychology, Giegerich is simply stating that the soul has "come into its own" as Subject, lying "within" our consciousness itself, beyond all substantial form (i.e. the logic of metaphysics). It is the objective within our subjectivity as I described it during my doctoral dissertation. See Giegerich, W. *What is Soul?* Op. cit. Pp. 257 ff.

68 "Understanding" here means our way of being, how we ordinarily comport ourselves pre-reflectively and intelligently in our world: See Heidegger's *Dasein*. For a concise introduction, see: Dreyfus, H., and Wrathall, M. (2005). "Martin Heidegger: An Introduction to His Thought, Work, and Life" in *A Companion to Heidegger* (Blackwell Companions to Philosophy, Vol. 29) (Kindle Locations 28-29). Kindle Edition.

69 See Index for all references to the psychological difference.

70 See Giegerich, W. (2013). *Neurosis: The Logic of a Metaphysical Illness.* New Orleans. Spring Journal Books.

71 See Edwards, J. C. (2008). "The Thinging of the Thing: The Ethic of Conditionality in Heidegger's Later Work" in *A Companion to Heidegger* (Blackwell Companions to Philosophy, Vol. 29) (Kindle Locations 8232). Kindle Edition.

72 Ibid. (Kindle Locations 8303-8305).

73 Ibid. (Kindle Locations 8276-8278).

74 Our world has always been linguistically constituted but only in modern times has this fact become conscious as philosophy turned to language itself. The question of language becoming conscious of itself, however, remains a profound mystery:

> [F]or we have now reached the fundamental level that we can call (with Johannes Lohmann) the "linguistic constitution of the world."! It presents itself as the consciousness that is effected by history . . . (Gadamer, H-G. *Philosophical Hermeneutics.* Op. cit. P. 13.)

75 Heidegger's momentous contribution to modern philosophy seems to have been to discover and articulate this world of background intelligibility, in which we cope prior to any reflection on our part.

His criticism that tradition (philosophy) has long ignored this world of *being* is based on the long-held distinction between being and "what-is" (the ontological difference). Over time, being was increasingly ignored, or was regarded as the *new* "what-is", meaning that we sacrificed *being* for the developing subject-object relationship that characterizes *knowing* (knowing *what* vs. knowing *how*). In terms of soul, we could say that as the historical soul separated from (what became) "the things", we turned the new status of soul into a "new thing" at the expense of its and our being. This is the history of metaphysics. Heidegger's existential phenomenology (world of Dasein) opens up the world in which we know *how*—pre-reflective knowledge, in an attempt to overcome the Cartesian subject-object form of knowing.

[76] To grasp this point fully would take very long discussion of the soul's view of history but everything said here is from the historical soul's point of view. See Giegerich, W. Chapter: "Alchemy of History" in *Soul Violence*. Op. cit.

[77] For a full discussion, see: Giegerich, W. (2007). *Technology and the Soul: From the Nuclear Bomb to the World Wide Web*. Spring Journal Books. New Orleans.

[78] This soul perspective on technological things seems to be very similar to Heidegger's concept of *bestand* which points to things that are completely replaceable and do not "gather" any "conditions" around them that, together, display a complete style of life, such as, say, an old handsaw might do. It does seem to me that "*bestand*" describes "things" that no longer carry soul, although Heidegger does not use this term. Instead he talks of "gathering the four-fold" which "der bestand" lacks.

[79] See Giegerich, W. (2005). *The Neurosis of Psychology*. Spring. New Orleans. P. 111.

[80] *How I Ended This Summer* (2011). This section is extracted from my book, Woodcock, J. C. *Animal Soul*. Op. cit.

[81] *Film Movement*. (2011, April 18). Retrieved from Film Movement: http://www.filmmovement.com with permission.

82 Giegerich, W. *Technology and the Soul: From the Nuclear Bomb to the World Wide Web.* Op. cit. P. 266.

83 See Guignon, C. (2005). "The History of Being" in *A Companion to Heidegger* (Blackwell Companions to Philosophy, Vol. 29) (Kindle Location 7052). Kindle Edition.

84 See: Carmen, T. (2005). "Authenticity" in *A Companion to Heidegger* (Blackwell Companions to Philosophy, Vol. 29) (Kindle Location 5121). Kindle Edition.

85 Giegerich, W. *Soul Violence.* Op. cit. P. 298 for the psychological difference:

> Archaic man not only lived "the psychological difference," the difference between human organism and soul, he *was*, which is much more, this difference in his very definition and *a priori*, whereas for us the psychological difference is inevitably no more than a *methodological* position we may at times take, and to take which requires, as experience shows, some effort and poses quite a few difficulties. . . . the psychological difference is for us always already superseded by our *a priori* being defined as positive fact, a biological organism, that merely *has* a psyche, a mind, and perhaps also "soul" and "spirit." The soul—this is our situation today—is inside us, and what is outside, the world, the cosmos, is a vis-à-vis for us.

86 Zweiter Band der "Psychoanalyse der Atombombe". Basel (Schweizer Spiegel Verlag, Raben-Reihe) 1989, S. 217-219. With thanks to R. F. Lukner, a member of ISPDI, for the translation that I have paraphrased. I remain solely responsible for this paraphrase of Giegerich's passage.

87 See my book, *The Imperative.* Op. cit. P. 39 ff.

88 See Giegerich, W. *The Soul Always Thinks.* Op. cit. P. 509n.

89 Lockhart, R. *Psyche Speaks.* Op. cit. P. 50.

90 Lockhart, R. (2013). "The Fictive Purpose of Dreams Part One: I Fear For the Dream" in *Dream Network Journal. Vol 32. No. 4.* http://www.understandthemeaningofmydreams.com/index.html.

91 This chapter is developed from my book, Woodcock, J. C. *Animal Soul.* Op. cit.

92 Jung, C. G. (ed. G. A. Adler, & tr. R. F. Hull). *C. G. Jung Letters (Vols. 2 (1951-1960)*. Op. cit. P. 591.

93 Image: Dennis L. Merritt © 2012. Permission granted.

94 This carving at Bollingen is referred to in Jaffe, A. (ed.) (1979). *C. G. Jung: Word and Image*. Op. cit. but has received scant attention until Russell Lockhart's book, *Psyche Speaks* was published in 1987. A comprehensive book on Jung's relation to art was published in 2012 and yet does not mention this carving specifically at all (van den Berk, T. (2012). *Jung on Art: The Autonomy of the Creative Drive*. New York. Psychology Press).

95 Jung, C. G. (ed. G. A. Adler, & tr. R. F. Hull). *C. G. Jung Letters (Vols. 2 (1951-1960)*. Op. cit. P. 615.

96 "[A]n event of soul is in truth the result of what happens when a dead letter and a human mind come together . . . The soul only comes alive in and by means of its dead productions." (Giegerich, W. *What is Soul?* Op. cit. P. 57-59).

97 See Jung, C. G., Jaffe, A. (ed.) and Winston, C; Winston, R. (trs). (1963). *Memories, Dreams, Reflections*. New York. Random House. Pp. 339-40.

98 Ibid. P. 78.

99 Giegerich, W. *The Soul Always Thinks*. Op. cit. P. 253.

100 Giegerich, W. *The Neurosis of Psychology*. Op. cit. P. 231.

101 Jung inscribed on the wall, in Latin, next to the mare nursing the woman: "May the light arise, which I have borne in my body." Also, see my "redeemer dream" above.

102 Lockhart, R. *Psyche Speaks*. Op. cit. Pp. 78-9.

103 Ibid. P. 74.

104 Giegerich, W. *The Soul Always Thinks*. Op. cit. P. 3.

105 Giegerich, W. *Soul Violence*. Op. cit. P. 298.

106 Giegerich, W. *The Soul Always Thinks*. Op. cit. P. 521.

107 Ibid. Pp.233 ff.

108 Iconic saying of Spock from *Star Trek*.

109 In particular I can draw attention to Giegerich's *explicit* recognition of the soul's downward movement into empirical reality:

> For at least 2,500 years the basic striving of Western man has been in the direction of the movement of this tale [of Plato's Cave—my insert]: away from the shadows to the real truth. But today, I think, we are witnessing the opposite movement, the soul's downward movement into the cave with the intent of settling there. Plato's cave never existed literally. It was a fiction for man to push off from. It seems that the striving today is to give this fiction a *literal* reality, for the first time. When we watch television in our living rooms, have we not almost literally become Platonic cave-dwellers, staring at the images coming from the TV, the shadows of the real world out there? Are we not, as if in fetters, captivated by what we are see and unable to pull away? (Giegerich, W. *Technology and the Soul*. Op. cit. Pp. 307-8.)

Giegerich goes on to further describe this downward soul gesture as:

> [the soul's—my insert] attempt at the intramundane realization of "the transmundane" or "transcendence," an attempt to represent atemporality or "eternity" *under the conditions of* empirical reality, an attempt at the *logical* overcoming of "the flesh" in the medium of "the flesh" and while being in "the flesh"—in favor of a presence of the spirit. (Ibid. P. 329.)

By "flesh", Giegerich is referring not to human bodies but "sarx": a positivistically conceived existence, a realization of Logos, the Idea, i.e., our positive, technological reality. Ibid. Pp. 178-80.

110 For some years I remained confused by Giegerich's privileging the upward soul gesture within the methodology of his psychology, while, in his writings he so often refers to the downward soul gesture with equal theoretical weight (see my Chapter: "Postscript"). Another example:

> When we look at psychological phenomenology we can see that there are two very different, even opposite intentionalities [what I call soul gestures—jw], *concerning what "the soul" wants to bring about in humans* . . . The need to be born into the world, to obtain a real empirical presence in life, to display itself: the soul's *anima* need [the downward soul gesture—my insert] [and] the need of the soul's further-determination the need to overcome and

John C. Woodcock

redefine itself: the soul's *animus* need [the upward soul gesture—my insert]. (Giegerich, W. *What is Soul?* Op. cit. P. 317-8.)

Yet, in his chosen art form, Giegerich privileges only the upward soul gesture i.e., the work of the human being to rise up to the level of soul and to think its logical life as that life thinks itself out in her. While he clearly affirms the reality of the downward soul gesture today, he offers no *methodology* for human participation in this downward movement by which the coming guest may arrive in its redeemed form rather than its present soulless and mechanical form (See my Chapter: "Postscript" for a qualification of this assertion of mine).

My first attempts to discuss Giegerich's methodologically exclusive valence towards the upward gesture were met with a "portcullis coming down and a drawbridge going up" as I wrote earlier. I concluded that this exclusion was not so much an argued position since, as I have shown, Giegerich does indeed give equal *theoretical* weight to both soul gestures. I concluded that the methodological exclusion of the downward gesture from psychology as a discipline of interiority had to do with Giegerich's "personal equation", i.e., it was a programmatic exclusion.

Whereas C. G. Jung gives us much biographical material from which subsequent scholars may draw conclusions concerning Jung's "personal equation" as expressed in his theoretical work, Giegerich give us no biographical access at all. Yet Giegerich insists himself that the personal equation is inevitable in *any* theory:

Each psychological interpretation or theoretical statement is at once also a self-representation of the psychologist. In what I say about my patients, I inevitably betray who I am . . . . Psychology is unavoidably confessional . . . .

The embarrassing thing about psychology is that in it one's professional identity is inevitably contaminated with one's personality. Psychology is nothing pure. My professional work, which I of course claim has a certain objective validity, is not only *de facto*, as all human endeavours, but also systematically infused with my personal equation inasmuch as I profess to be a Jungian or whatever. (Giegerich, W. *The Neurosis of Psychology.* Op. cit. P. 153-4.)

Based on what Giegerich says about his own psychology, then, we may therefore discern, implicitly at least, the presence, if not the content, of *his* personal equation too! And I think it lies in what I call his *programmatic* exclusion of any *methodological* consideration w.r.t the downward soul gesture, a gesture that also demands human participation, i.e., the kind of participation that Lockhart examines in his book, *Psyche Speaks* (Op. cit.).

111 Lockhart, R. *Psyche Speaks.* Op. cit. P. 76.

112 See Giegerich, W. "Jung's Thought of the Self" in *The Neurosis of Psychology.* Op. cit. Pp. 171 ff.

113 See n. 109 above where Giegerich also invokes the metaphor of birth in relation to the downward soul gesture: the soul's need *to be born* into the world, etc.

114 Lockhart, R. *Psyche Speaks.* Op. cit. P. 79. All these "acts" presuppose an ego that is capable of taking responsibility for its actions.

115 Lockhart, R. *Psyche Speaks.* Op. cit. P. 34.

116 Although, as I said above, Giegerich offers no method for participation by the human being in the downward soul gesture (the incarnation of the coming guest in the empirical world) he does offer some pertinent hints as to the nature of any art form that so seeks to express the downward soul gesture. See my Chapter: "Postscript".

117 That is to say, the author may imaginatively *describe* the process of actualization of the coming guest through the empirical person, but may not have had the experience themselves of that process (c/f Jung and the writing of *The Red Book* which clearly shows that his account is autobiographical. He wrote it as it happened to him. This is the germ of the new art form.)

118 Lewis, C. S. (2012, 11 29). *C. S. Lewis Lectures on the Novels of Charles Williams.* Retrieved from YouTube: https://www.youtube.com/watch?v=Z5w134gYz04.

119 See my book, *Overcoming Solidity.* Op. cit. Chapter: "Individual Experience of Overcoming Solidity".

120 Lockhart, R. A. *Psyche Speaks.* Op. cit. P. 37.

121 See especially my books: Woodcock, J. C. *Overcoming Solidity: World Crisis and the New Nature.* Op. cit. and *Manifesting Possible Futures.* Op. cit. Chapter: "Tarning and Literature".

122   For a discussion of the world-creating meaning of "event", see Heidegger and his notion of Ereignis:

   The responsible way to gain a sense of Ereignis is to combine close reading with independent thought. We must trace the word's roles in crucial texts while keeping in mind its usual meaning, corresponding to the English "event." . . . As we will see, in 1919 it means, roughly, a kind of experience in which I find myself intimately involved, as opposed to an experience in which I am nothing but an objective viewer. In 1936-8 it means, roughly, the possible happening in which a new dwelling may be founded—a place and age in which a people could cultivate significance. [Polt, R. (2005). "Ereignis" in *A Companion to Heidegger*. Op. cit. (Kindle Locations 6750-6755)]

123   The following is excerpted from a longer discussion in my book, Woodcock, J. C. *Making New Worlds: The Way of the Artist*. Op. cit.

124   Jung, C. G. *Nietzsche's Zarathustra*. Op. cit.

125   See Jung, C. G. *Memories, Dreams, Reflections*. Op. cit. Chapter: "Confrontation with the Unconscious".

126   Jung, C. G. *Nietzsche's Zarathustra*. Op. cit. P. 184 ff.

127   Kerenyi, K. (1990). *Hermes: Guide of Souls*. Dallas. Spring Journal Books. P. 88.

128   Heidegger, M., Hertz, P. D. (tr.) (1971). *On the Way to Language*. San Francisco. Harper San Francisco. Pp. 73-75.

129   Jung, C. G. *Nietzsche's Zarathustra*. Op. cit. Pp. 187-197.

130   A significant exception lies in the work of Wolfgang Giegerich who writes about Jung's ordeal: "A prolonged step-by-step process of sinking the form of thought into the form of the individual's . . . existential experience 'in the flesh.'" Giegerich evaluates this process in terms of its neurotic structure, i.e. the psychological difference not seen as such by Jung. This negative evaluation is in accord with Giegerich's valorising only the upward gesture of the modern soul and is aimed at Jung the psychologist, whereas Jung as artist of the soul was participating in the downward gesture of the soul into actuality. See Giegerich, W. (2010). "Liber Novis, that is, The New Bible, A First Analysis of C. G. Jung's Red Book". *Spring 83: Minding The Animal Psyche*. New Orleans. Spring Journal. Pp. 391-2 ff.

131 Woodcock, J. C. *Making New Worlds*. Chapter: "The Violent Character of the New Art Form". Op. cit.

132 Jung, C. G., Shamdasani, S.(ed.) (2009). *The Red Book*. New York. Norton. P. 290.

133 See Jung, C. G. *Memories, Dreams, Reflections*. Op. cit. Chapter: "Confrontation with the Unconscious" for Jung's account of this penetration of the objective psyche into empirical reality.

134 Jung, C. G. *Analytical Psychology*. Op. cit. P. 96-97. This is Jung's experience of the *Leontocephalus* which has attracted attention in the secondary literature for the purpose of challenging or affirming Jung's concept of the collective unconscious. See, for example, Noll, R. (1992). "Jung the Leontocephalus", *Spring 53*. Putnam. Spring Journal. Pp. 12-60, and Mogenson's rebuttal: Mogenson, G. (1994). "The Collective Unconscious and the Leontocephalus: A Rejoinder to Noll". Letter to the Editor, *Spring 56*: Putnam. Spring Journal. Pp. 132-137. In this rebuttal, Mogenson notes that for Jung: "It was not the parrellism of the imagery that was of archetypal significance, but his living experience of its numinous power. It was the fact that he experienced an initiation and felt himself to be transformed that was important, not his having been transfigured into the lion-headed deity, Leontocephalus." It is in this passage that Mogenson notes, without grasping its significance for the new art form, that Jung is saying that he [Jung] was *initiated*, in his empirical reality, by a purely fictional reality!

135 I describe similar personal experiences in: Woodcock, J. C. *The Imperative*. Op. cit. Pp. 18 ff.

136 See Woodcock, J. C. *Making New Worlds*. Op. cit.

137 Ibid.

138 See Woodcock, J. C. *Overcoming Solidity*. Op.Cit. Chapter: "The Problem and its Philosophical Background" for a brief discussion of the history of this rupture.

139 "Art-life" is a linguistic contrivance like "psycho-somatic" and in no way implies the achievement of such unity.

140 Smith, T. (2011). *Contemporary Art: World Currents*. London: Laurence King Publishing. P. 9.

141 For an in-depth discussion of art as "world-configuring", see Dreyfus, H. (2005). "Heidegger's Ontology of Art" in *A Companion to Heidegger*. Op. cit. Kindle Location 7325.

142 http://www.youtube.com/watch?v=316AzLYfAzw

143 See Dreyfus, H. *Being-in-the-World*. Chapter: "The 'Who' of Everyday Dasein". Op. cit.

144 Giegerich, W. *Technology and the Soul*. Op. cit. Pp. 255-6.

145 Ibid. Pp. 253-4.

146 See n. 14.

147 Giegerich, W. *The Soul's Logical Life*. Op. cit. P. 243.

148 "Participation," not "experience", i.e., overcoming the habitual subject-object form of consciousness:

> [A] soul truth . . . is neither a metaphysical claim nor can it be experienced . . . something very real, . . . but it cannot be an experience, inasmuch as it is something syntactical, and not something semantic . . . . And just as the syntax of a given language can be analysed, so the logical or syntactical form of real soul phenomena is (and must be) analyzable, demonstrable, communicable, not only an inner experience beyond speech. (Giegerich, W. *C. G. Jung on Christianity and on Hegel*. Op. cit. Pp. 212-14)

149 See my *Foreword to the Second Edition* above for a discussion of the redeemed form of the coming guest.

150 See Introduction for a discussion of "punctum".

151 During my life, I exhibited a persistent longing to submit fully to external authority, in one form or another. Invariably such submission was undermined, with incredible disappointment or feelings of betrayal on my part. It now seems to me that this "failure" was a necessary movement towards interiorizing the whole issue of submission to authority, as this dream shows.

152 Giegerich, W. *C. G. Jung on Christianity and on Hegel*. Op. cit. P. 15.

153 Ibid. P. 216.

154 Owen Barfield, following S. T. Coleridge, explores the historical relationship between thinking and perception in terms of the difference between dividing (separating) and distinguishing:

> One of the most valuable lessons I learned from Coleridge was to detect that terribly obsessive, and terribly contemporary, fallacy which supposes that we must only *distinguish* things that we are also able to *divide*. It is closely allied to an obsession with space as the criterion of reality. When we divide things, we set them, either in fact or imagination, side by side in space. But space is not the be-all and end-all, and there are many things that, by reason of their interpenetration . . . cannot be divided, though they are easily distinguished: acquaintance and friendship . . . thinking and perceiving . . . . [Barfield, O. (1979). *History, Guilt, and Habit.* Irvington. Columbia University Press. P. 11 ff.]

155 Gadamer, H. G. *Truth and Method.* Op. cit. See my book, *Making New Worlds. Chapter: The Herm* for another account of the downward soul gesture which led me into an in-depth study of Heidegger and hermeneutics. Op. cit.

156 Gadamer, H. G. *Truth and Method.* Op. cit. P. 107.

157 Ibid. P. 369.

158 Ibid. P. 386.

159 Giegerich, W. C. G. *Jung on Christianity and on Hegel.* Op. cit. P. 216.

160 Gadamer, H. G. *Truth and Method.* Op. cit. P. 369.

161 See my *Foreword to the Second Edition* above, for a discussion of the "mechanical and soulless" form of the coming guest.

162 Poem by author. Complete poems on death may be found in my book, Woodcock, J. (2013). *Ur-image.* Bloomington. iUniverse. These poems are also the result of my following the downward soul gesture.

163 Giegerich, W. C. G. *Jung on Christianity and on Hegel.* Op. cit.

164 Ibid. P. 335.

165 This "devaluation of the image" throughout Giegerich's work has been noted by others in the Jungian community who valorize the image in the light of their project to "re-enchant" the world. But Giegerich's apparent devaluation of the image is simply a reflection of

his devotion to the modern soul which has *itself* devalued the image completely (see Giegerich, W. *Technology and the Soul.* Op. cit.)

166 We can see a rare and explicit example of Giegerich's programmatic refusal to consider the downward soul gesture methodologically, expressed by him in terms of his personal equation:

There is a legitimate place for the expression of one's "*feelings* of sorrow and grief" . . . as well as for all other feelings and private affairs. This place, I feel, is the privacy of "one's closet" *or* the privacy of one's relation to intimate friends, loved ones, family, analyst, priest. Maybe I am very old-fashioned . . . Nevertheless it offends my sense of propriety and of style if, in a *work* of thought (which as thought by its very nature belongs to the public domain . . .), the author enters with his or her personal feelings about his or her private affairs, where such confession is not necessitated by the inner logic of the subject matter at hand. I would call this indecent exposure. (Giegerich, W. *The Soul Always Thinks.* Op. cit. P. 128-9.)

On the same page Giegerich notes an exception, "A public place where intimate personal feelings may be expressed is art, lyric poetry. But this is something different. By having been transported into the "objective" medium of art, the merely personal has been detached from the privacy of the person and has received public status."

167 Giegerich, W. "Psychology as Anti-Philosophy: C. G. Jung." *Spring 77: Philosophy and Psychology.* New Orleans. Spring Journal. Pp. 11-51.

168 Jung, C. G. *Memories, Dreams, Reflections.* Op. cit. Pp.36 ff.

169 See Giegerich, W. (2005). *The Neurosis of Psychology.* Op. cit.

170 Giegerich, W. *Psychology as Anti-Philosophy: C. G. Jung.* Op. cit. P. 16.

171 It is important to note here that Giegerich shows how the fortuitous aspect (e.g. Jung's desire for personal salvation) is appropriated to the soul's need and thus has its necessity, too. There probably is a union of *telos* and contingency at work here.

172 Giegerich discusses the contrast between the ordinary modern person and the "great artist or thinker" at some length:

. . . those who are great artists, great philosophers, composers, or great in some other area of cultural production, those in whom, in addition to their ordinariness, soul happens, on the one hand, and those—that is, most of us—who are not "great", not seized by a cultural work or by the truth of the age, those who are only ordinary persons, only human, all-too-human, on the other hand . . . . The former give voice to the soul, the others circle around themselves as private individuals with their "claims to happiness, contentment and security in life". (Giegerich, W. *What is Soul?* Op. cit. P. 190.)

173   Giegerich, W. *Liber Novis, that is, The New Bible, A First Analysis of C. G. Jung's Red Book.* Op. cit. P. 392.

174   Ibid. P. 391.

175   Giegerich's exclusive valence towards the upward soul gesture is often expressed by him in alchemical terms:

> The great artist or thinker is no more than an alchemical vessel in which the great problems of the time are the prime matter undergoing their fermenting corruption, distillation, sublimation and of course articulation. And the real artifex of the work is ultimately the mercurial spirit stirring from within the *problems* of the age themselves. The great thinker and artist is thus he or she who can allow the Mercurius in the great questions of the age to do its stirring within himself or herself. (Giegerich, W. *The Soul Always Thinks.* Op. cit. P. 253.)

Here we can see that although Giegerich acknowledges the downward soul gesture ("articulation" by the great artist) he methodologically valorises only the upward soul gesture, in accordance with his goal of making soul or psychology (reaching the soul in the Real today). But this valorisation so often is accompanied by his devaluation of the downward soul gesture, leading to challenges such as that by Stanton Marlan who "seek(s) to express psyche's need to *substantiate* [my italics]":

> Hillman has noted that depth psychology, including Jung's, has had difficulty in finding a way to express the complex/simplicity of psyche's need to substantiate or likewise of substance's need to speak. For Hillman, the problematic is in part rooted in the way conceptual language splits apart a fundamental unity, "abstracting matter from image." When this occurs, there is a powerful psychic demand to heal the split, to substantiate psyche and to bring it back in touch with something solid. The problem of languaging the soul was present for Jung throughout his life and work. The need to substantiate, to go beyond words and paper, played a role in his desire

to personify and in his urge to turn to stone. [Marlan, S. (2006). "From the Black Sun to the Philosopher's Stone" in *Spring 74: Alchemy*. P. 17-18 and P. 24.]

176 To add to the complexity of Giegerich's thought re: the new art form as an expression of the coming guest, I discovered some passages in his latest book, *C. G. Jung on Christianity and on Hegel* (op. cit.), that point to our current *lack of* any (art?) form that expresses our current psychological condition in modernity. There Giegerich draws our attention to *styles of writing*:

> [As a writer, Jung's style] was immediately and effortlessly accessible to ordinary conventional consciousness . . . . Jung did not demand of his readers *to actively participate in producing a new sensibility, in a new way of assuming responsibilities to the world and to each other.* (P. 362)

In other words, Giegerich is questioning the *form* of Jung's style of writing as an art form that can in effect initiate the reader into the inner logic of modernity as which we exist! He compares the inadequacy of Jung's style (which remains as the logic of metaphysics, under modern conditions of positivity) to that of Hegel:

> Hegel . . . addressed the problem where it really was . . . His language was laborious because he demanded of the reader—of *consciousness*—to undertake the personal effort to become adequate in its very constitution to this higher complexity, to feel responsible for the new sensibility required by the modern situation. He knew that what was needed was an *education* of *consciousness*. His language style aimed at the *form* of consciousness (instead of merely providing, like Jung, new edifying contents or experiences for it: archetypal, numinous images). (P. 377)

Giegerich appears to be pointing to the need (by asserting its current absence) for an art form (here literature) that, *in its form*, mirrors or expresses the structure of modern soul (absolute negativity, the formal relations that go by the name of the psychological difference, pure thinking etc.)

In these passages I see a wealth of hints for a new art form that seeks to participate in the incarnation of the coming guest in its *redeemed* form in the material world.

177 We can see the enormous difference in the "violence" of penetration by the objective psyche in Jung the *artist* by comparing his reported

experiences during the time of *The Red Book* with those when, near the end of his life, he carved the high relief into the wall at Bollingen. I strongly suspect that the difference can be accounted for by a softening of Jung's wilfulness over time and corresponding opening of the heart to the presence of the coming guest.

178 The *Red Book* is composed of Jung's active imaginations, along with his Commentaries in which he later tried to understand his experience from an external point of view. These later deliberations formed the basis of his theoretical work as a psychologist.

179 In terms of the new art form and the artist's participation in the downward soul gesture, we can see that in each of the three examples of active imagination cited here, "a route back into literal and material reality" was accomplished: a carving, *The Red Book*, and in the case of his early active imagination, an *achievement* (i.e. in the empirical world): "My one great achievement during those years [subsequent to his vision] was that I resisted the temptation to talk about it with anyone" (see *Memories, Dreams, Reflections*, op. cit. P. 41). Since I am proposing that active imagination, i.e. the kind Jung practiced, demonstrates the germ of the method of a new art form, we may ask if we can apprehend the coming guest, in its redeemed form, as the inwardness of all three examples cited here. Are all three products the material residues ("dead letters") of a manifestation of spiritual love, through Jung the artist? Giegerich clearly shows that Jung's psychology is indeed a manifestation in the real world of the soul's need, in this case its neurotic need to bring home and make explicit to itself its overcoming of its own form as metaphysical logic.

180 Giegerich, W. *C. G. Jung on Christianity and on Hegel.* Op. cit. P. 43.

181 Lockhart, R. *Psyche Speaks.* Op. cit. P. 22. He is here partially quoting Cary Baynes.